MARKETING
6.0

PHILIP KOTLER
HERMAWAN KARTAJAYA
IWAN SETIAWAN

MARKETING
6.0

THE FUTURE IS IMMERSIVE

WILEY

Library of Congress Cataloging-in-Publication Data is Available:

ISBN 9781119835219 (Cloth)
ISBN 9781119835370 (ePub)
ISBN 9781119835387 (ePDF)

Cover Design: Wiley
Cover Image: © Marketeers
Author Photo: Courtesy of the Authors

SKY10087407_100924

Marketing's purpose always is to enhance people's lives and contribute to the common good.

—Philip Kotler

To my son, Michael, daughter, Stephanie, and grandson, Darren: I hope they will become the next-generation creators of immersive experiences.

—Hermawan Kartajaya

Dedicated to my beloved family: Louise, Jovin, and Justin.

—Iwan Setiawan

Contents

PART I

Introduction to Marketing 6.0

CHAPTER 1

Welcoming the Era of Marketing 6.0

From Multi to Omni to Meta

The *Marketing X.0* book series explores the shifts in the business landscape and how those shifts would change how marketers approach marketing. The first installment, *Marketing 3.0: From Products to Customers to the Human Spirit*, examines how marketing has come full circle in its evolution to serve humanity. In Marketing 3.0, customers look for not only functional and emotional satisfaction but also spiritual fulfillment from the brands they choose. As the subtitle suggests, the book describes the major shifts from product-driven marketing (1.0) to customer-oriented marketing (2.0) to human-centric marketing (3.0).

Very forward-looking at the time of its publication in 2010, the book provided a blueprint for engaging modern customers seeking to do business with companies that positively impact society. Today, incorporating sustainability themes in marketing is crucial to remain relevant, particularly in light of the United Nations' Sustainable Development Goals (SDGs). By aligning their marketing with the SDGs, businesses can demonstrate their commitment to solving humanity's biggest problems.

One of the key roles of marketing is to communicate value and build trust with the customers, allowing brands to influence behaviors. Procter & Gamble, for example, is leveraging its massive share of voice to drive change through marketing. One of the world's largest advertisers, P&G advocates diversity, equity, and inclusion themes in its successful storytelling campaigns for brands such as Gillette, Always, and Pampers.

Marketing is also responsible for expanding the market and driving growth. When products and services reach underserved markets, we are one step closer to a fully inclusive society—the overarching agenda of SDGs.

A compelling example is the Next Billion Users program, where Google creates suitable technology products for first-time, inexperienced Internet users. With the ability to understand the market, develop relevant products, and drive technology adoption, Google is well equipped to achieve this objective. One such product is Google Lens, which can read words aloud to illiterate individuals in developing countries.

As technology continues to evolve, it changes how marketers interact with customers. The second book, *Marketing 4.0: Moving from Traditional to Digital,* was again ahead of its time, encouraging businesses to adapt to the increasingly digital landscape and engage the digital-savvy generations to make them loyal advocates.

Marketing 4.0 took inspiration from Industry 4.0, which epitomized the movement toward digital. Introduced as a high-level strategy of the German government in 2011, Industry 4.0—the fourth industrial revolution—outlines the development of manufacturing systems in adopting digital technologies.

Marketing 4.0 stressed the importance of experimenting with digital marketing to complement the traditional approach across the customer journey. Adopting digital strategies such as content marketing and omnichannel marketing has become imperative.

Content marketing involves creating and sharing valuable content with a target audience, primarily through social media. It is more effective than traditional advertising because the content is typically more relevant and engaging than ads. The approach is usually paired with omnichannel marketing, the process of integrating online and offline channels to create a seamless customer experience. Those two paradigms have proven to be particularly relevant and valuable for marketers navigating the unforeseeable challenges of the pandemic.

During the two years of the pandemic, two-thirds of local businesses used content marketing, increasing total spending by nearly $20 billion—according to Meta Branded Content Project. Similarly, Square and the Atlantic reported that more than 75 percent of businesses across sectors—retail, health and fitness, restaurants, home and repair, and professional services—implemented omnichannel marketing.

While content marketing and omnichannel approach have today become essential staples of digital strategy, recent technological advances are taking us to the next level. The cornerstone technology discussed in *Marketing 5.0: Technology for Humanity* is artificial intelligence (AI), which aims to replicate human capability in solving problems and making decisions.

Marketing 5.0 took inspiration from Society 5.0, which introduces the theme of leveraging technology for humanity. Society 5.0 was introduced by the Japanese government in 2016 as a natural progression from Industry 4.0. It envisioned a society that leverages advanced technology, such as AI, for the good of humanity.

During over 60 years of its history, AI has created polarizing opinions. Businesspeople have been wary of the threat of AI, from the loss of jobs to the extinction of humanity. Yet, despite fears and anxieties brought forth by AI, the benefits for humanity are apparent. With its capacity to analyze large volumes of data, predict future outcomes, and deliver personalized experiences at scale, AI is rapidly changing how companies run their businesses.

A case in point is PepsiCo, which collects insights on potential flavors and new product categories based on digital data—social media posts and online recipe commentaries—and analyzes them with AI. Products created with AI insights include Off The Eaten Path snacks and Propel sports drinks. At PepsiCo, AI rapidly shifted from experimental to applied technology for product development.

AI, too, has advanced significantly since the *Marketing 5.0* publication. Achieving artificial general intelligence (AGI), which has humanlike cognitive capabilities, is still a complex and challenging goal, but many are working to advance the field. AI today is far more interactive and mainstream. OpenAI's ChatGPT represents a promising step forward for AI. ChatGPT, as a highly intelligent and interactive language model, can facilitate communication between humans and machines, enabling more effective collaboration.

The developments of AI have enabled a group of other technologies to advance, changing the business landscape once more and thus driving the next evolution of marketing.

The Rise of Immersive Marketing 6.0

There has been a notable shift in technological advancements in recent years toward creating more immersive interactions between customers and brands. This shift can be attributed to the rise of the digital native generations, namely Generation Z and Generation Alpha, who were born into a world where the Internet was already prevalent. These younger cohorts have a strong affinity for immersive experiences that blend physical and digital elements. We will delve deeper into the characteristics and preferences of these two cohorts in Chapter 2.

The emergence of these generations will bring about significant changes to the digital landscape, transforming various aspects of the digital space. One notable transformation is the increasing interactivity and immersion within the digital realm. A prime example of this is the prevalence of short-form videos on social media that captivate audiences, leading to endless scrolling and an immersive viewing experience. Moreover, e-commerce has become more engaging, featuring innovative models that facilitate conversations between buyers and sellers through chats and livestreams. Chapter 3 will delve into these emerging trends and their impact on the digital space.

These trends inspire businesses to provide increasingly immersive customer experiences that blur the lines between physical and digital touchpoints. By combining the advantages of offline interactions, such as multisensory experiences and human-to-human engagement, with the benefits of online experiences, which include personalized interactions on a larger scale, companies can create truly immersive customer journeys. We believe that post-pandemic, a significant portion of customer experiences will continue to occur in physical spaces. However, there is a growing trend of augmenting these physical interactions with digital technologies to cater to the needs of the digital native generations. We discuss this theme in greater detail in Chapter 4.

Two prominent technologies that facilitate the augmentation of physical spaces with digital elements are augmented reality (AR) and virtual reality (VR). While both technologies blend the physical and digital realms, their approach differs. AR incorporates digital elements into the real world, enhancing the physical environment with digital overlays. This allows users to experience the physical surroundings while interacting with digital content. On the other hand, VR creates entirely virtual environments, completely immersing users in a digital world detached from their physical surroundings.

AR finds widespread application in games such as Pokémon Go, where players can find and capture virtual monsters that seem to inhabit real-world locations when viewed through mobile phone screens. Businesses have also embraced AR extensively. For example, IKEA offers customers the ability to virtually place furniture in their homes using its mobile app before making a purchase. Similarly, L'Oréal utilizes AR technology to provide virtual makeup try-on experiences, generating digital images that make it appear as if customers are wearing makeup.

On the other hand, VR takes immersion to the next level. Customers can fully immerse themselves in virtual environments that closely simulate real-world experiences. Companies including Volvo and BMW utilize VR for virtual test drives, while *The New York Times* employs VR to deliver stories with rich multimedia content. Both AR and VR fall under the broader concept of extended reality (XR), which enables users to consume digital experiences within physical spaces.

Conversely, some technologies enable users to feel like they are experiencing real-world sensations in a digital environment. This concept is called the metaverse, representing the other side of the immersive experience. In simple terms, a metaverse means a virtual world closely resembling the physical world.

The early forms of metaverses originated from the gaming industry, with popular virtual-world games such as Roblox, Fortnite, Minecraft, Decentraland, and The Sandbox. These virtual environments even offer non-gaming experiences, such as hosting musical concerts for artists including Marshmello, Travis Scott, and Ariana Grande within Fortnite. However, the concept of a metaverse is not limited to gaming and entertainment, as it has the potential to be the immersive version of social media for younger generations.

Both XR and the metaverse eliminate the boundaries between the physical and digital realms, resulting in a highly immersive experience. We called this "metamarketing," the cornerstone of Marketing 6.0. The prefix "meta" is derived from Greek and means "beyond" or "transcending." Therefore, metamarketing is defined as a marketing approach

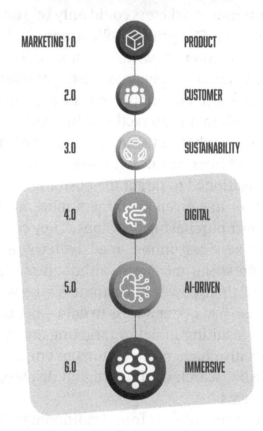

FIGURE 1.1　The Evolution of Marketing.

that transcends the boundaries between the physical and digital worlds, providing an immersive experience where customers perceive no distinction between the two (see Figure 1.1).

Metamarketing as the Next Stage of Omnichannel Marketing

Before the Internet, marketers could only rely on traditional channels such as TV, print publications, and brick-and-mortar stores to interact with customers. Thus, marketing had been about engaging specific market segments through their most commonly consumed media paired with human-to-human interactions. But with the information asymmetry—where customers had limited access to information and interactions with one another—marketers were better positioned to target the customers.

The Internet has given customers more media choices and control over purchasing decisions. They could research products and services online, read reviews, and connect with others on social media. So although marketers were losing some of their power to customers who were gaining power, they also had better access to data—because of more effective AI—resulting in better targeting and accountability. Marketers also have more options to engage customers via social media, search engines, digital displays, and even gaming platforms.

It is not a complete shift from traditional to digital marketing, however. At least not yet. Despite the mainstream use of the Internet and several years of the pandemic, most customers still find the human touch appealing. E-commerce was only approximately 15 percent of total retail sales in the United States in 2022, according to the US Department of Commerce. Euromonitor estimates that e-commerce penetration is much larger—and the highest globally—in China but still below 30 percent.

As a result, businesses cannot simply switch from traditional to digital marketing. Instead, they have explored ways to utilize both conventional and digital channels. In its 2022 Chief Marketing Officer (CMO) Survey in North America and Europe, Gartner estimated that 56 percent of the marketing budget was spent on digital while the rest was still allocated to offline channels.

Thus, two of the most popular marketing concepts in recent years are multichannel and omnichannel. Both have become crucial in providing a convenient customer experience, allowing companies to engage with their target audience online and offline. They also reflect the ongoing trend of traditional and digital marketing convergence, as discussed in the books *Marketing 4.0* and *Marketing 5.0*.

Multichannel marketing is a strategy where a company uses multiple channels to promote its products or services. These channels may include a mix of traditional and digital media. The goal is to increase a brand's visibility and reach a wider audience. Still, each medium is often used independently, with different messaging and objectives. The assumption is that traditional and digital customers go through separate journeys, and businesses must interact with them with two different customer experiences.

As a case in point, a beverage company could use multichannel marketing to target older and younger generations. It might use TV ads during daytime and evening programs to target older audiences with messaging focused on health benefits. For a younger audience, the company could use Instagram with messaging around trendy flavors and convenience.

In recent years, however, marketers realized that modern customers often interact with businesses online and offline in a single marketing funnel. Moreover, online and offline channels sometimes complement more than substitute. For example, in the automotive sector, online channels are effective for search and product discovery but less for product evaluations and purchases. That is where omnichannel marketing comes in.

Omnichannel marketing is a more integrated approach where a company creates a seamless customer experience across all channels. Customers can interact with the brand through any channel, such as a physical store, social media, website, or mobile app, and receive a consistent message and experience. Each channel can play a different role in driving customers throughout the entire path to purchase.

For example, consider how webrooming compares to showrooming. In a webrooming scenario, a customer researches products online before purchasing in a physical store. Take, for instance, consumer electronics. A customer might explore a new smartphone or laptop online before going to a physical store to evaluate the product in person and make a final decision. In this case, online media play a significant role at the top of the funnel, while the offline channel is at the bottom of the marketing funnel.

However, in the showrooming scenario, the role of traditional and digital media is reversed. In fashion retailing, for example, customers often visit physical stores to try on clothing and see how it fits before purchasing online for better prices and complete colorways. The media mix is traditional on the upper funnel and digital at the bottom.

Marketers consider omnichannel marketing a step up from the multichannel approach because it enables businesses to create a seamless customer journey, regardless of how customers interact with the brand. By understanding the roles that different channels play in the path to purchase, businesses can provide a consistent message and experience across all channels and better serve their customers. This, in turn, can improve their overall marketing efforts and increase customer loyalty.

As marketing continues to evolve, we are looking beyond omnichannel marketing to a new approach called metamarketing. Metamarketing takes a step beyond omnichannel by providing an interactive and immersive approach to delivering customer experience. Like multichannel and omnichannel marketing, metamarketing is about unifying physical and digital customer experience.

While multichannel marketing provides customers with online and offline channels based on their preferences, and omnichannel marketing integrates physical and digital touchpoints for a seamless experience, metamarketing strives to create a fully immersive customer journey (see Figure 1.2). It involves delivering digital experiences in physical spaces or providing real-life experiences in virtual environments—realizing the ultimate convergence of the physical and digital realms. Although still a relatively new concept, metamarketing shows great potential for businesses seeking to stay ahead of the curve.

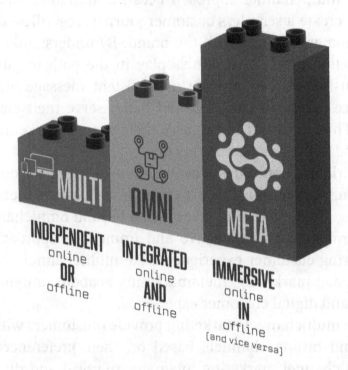

META IS THE NEXT STAGE OF OMNI

MULTI
INDEPENDENT
online
OR
offline

OMNI
INTEGRATED
online
AND
offline

META
IMMERSIVE
online
IN
offline
[and vice versa]

FIGURE 1.2   The Traditional and Digital Marketing Convergence.

The Building Blocks of Marketing 6.0

Marketing 6.0, or metamarketing, covers a range of strategies and tactics that enable companies to deliver immersive experiences across physical and digital media. To achieve this, Marketing 6.0 relies on several essential building blocks organized into three distinct layers.

The first layer, which serves as the foundation, comprises technological enablers that blend physical and digital experiences. These technologies provide the groundwork for the second layer, which consists of two distinct environments: extended realities and metaverses. Extended realities refer to digitally augmented physical spaces, while metaverses are virtual worlds that offer experiences closely resembling real life. Lastly, the third and top layer encompasses customer-facing experiences, characterized by multisensory engagement (involving all five senses), spatial (3D) digital experiences, and marketing within metaverses (virtual worlds) (see Figure 1.3).

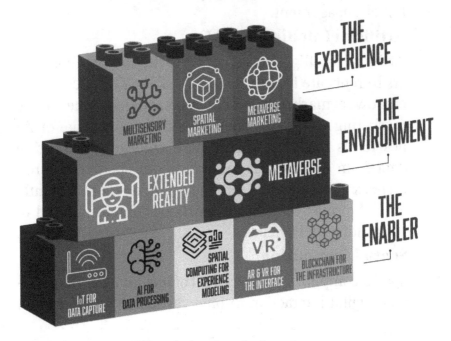

FIGURE 1.3 The Building Blocks of Marketing 6.0.

The Enabler Layer

Marketing 6.0 is powered by five advanced technologies increasingly adopted by businesses across sectors (explored more in Chapter 5).

- **The Internet of Things (IoT)**

  IoT refers to interconnected sensors that capture real-time data from the physical environment and transform it into valuable digital information for marketers. For example, IoT technology can detect customers' movements in retail stores. This enables retailers to deliver in-app promotion notifications instantly, triggered by shoppers as they stroll down specific store aisles. By leveraging IoT, businesses can enhance their marketing strategies by utilizing timely and location-based customer engagement.

- **Artificial Intelligence (AI)**

  Artificial intelligence (AI) refers to the ability of computers to replicate human cognitive skills. This technology empowers marketers to deliver personalized one-to-one marketing strategies. The remarkable advantage of AI lies in its real-time capabilities, constantly capturing data from IoT sources to learn about customers' preferences and behaviors, enabling marketers to instantly offer the most relevant products or content tailored to each individual's needs.

- **Spatial Computing**

  Spatial computing involves a set of technologies that facilitate digital interaction in physical space. Its application in retail stores, such as implementing smart fitting rooms, enhances the shopping experience by offering customers interactivity and immersion. These smart fitting rooms can instantly identify the clothing items customers bring in, provide personalized styling recommendations, and enable virtual try-on. Spatial computing is pivotal in allowing this unique fusion of digital and physical experiences.

- **AR and VR**

  AR and VR technologies are revolutionizing how we engage with digital content. AR provides customers an interactive and immersive experience by enabling them to explore products virtually and visualize how they appear and function in real-life environments. For example, customers can try on shoes virtually to see how they would look on their feet. On the other hand, VR is utilized for practical training purposes, such as training customer service representatives through hands-on simulations and scenarios.

- **Blockchain**

  Blockchain is a groundbreaking technology that paves the way for a decentralized Internet. It empowers content creators to have ownership over the content they produce, eliminating the reliance on centralized social media platforms. This technology serves as the foundation for community-driven metaverses, where content and governance are owned and controlled by a community of users. With blockchain, metaverses can establish robust economies, complete with their own currency and commerce systems for seamless virtual goods transactions.

The Environment Layer

Marketing 6.0 revolves around creating immersive environments in both the physical and digital realms. While physical spaces will continue to be the primary avenue for delivering customer experiences, businesses must reimagine these spaces by incorporating digital experiences to ensure their future relevance. We refer to these digitally enhanced physical spaces as "extended realities," acknowledging the XR technologies that enable such augmentation.

Digital technologies bring a new level of immersion to physical spaces, allowing companies to streamline transactions and provide quick, seamless checkouts similar to e-commerce sites. Additionally, these technologies enable more personalized engagements through interactive displays. Marketers can engage shoppers with multiple screens displaying customized recommendations and interactive touchscreen capabilities.

Furthermore, digital technologies allow customers to discover products in novel ways, transforming in-store research into an engaging experience. One approach involves the use of mobile apps equipped with in-store modes. These apps enable customers to scan QR codes next to each product, granting them access to comprehensive information and details about the products. A detailed exploration of these digital enhancements will be presented in Chapter 6.

In Marketing 6.0, we also delve into the exploration of the metaverse. The metaverse refers to fully functional virtual worlds that bear similarities to the real world. Avatars represent individuals, and virtual assets resemble physical objects within these virtual environments. The metaverse is considered the latest form of social media, attracting the attention and engagement of Generation Z and Generation Alpha.

The metaverse can be categorized into two distinct types: decentralized and centralized. Decentralized metaverses operate under the governance of a community of users connected through blockchain technology. On the other hand, centralized metaverses are managed by a single entity. While doubts and skepticism continue to exist, particularly surrounding the decentralized metaverse, its potential to transform how businesses provide immersive customer experiences should not be underestimated.

The Experience Layer

In the Marketing 6.0 era, marketers can provide three distinct types of experiences, which we explore in-depth in Chapters 8–10. The first type is the multisensory marketing experience. Engaging customers' five senses through multisensory marketing can be a powerful tool to evoke positive emotions and influence behavior. Companies such as Starbucks have been leveraging this approach for years, with visually appealing stores, music playlists, signature coffee smells and tastes, and comfortable seating and cups.

However, with the rise of digital media, multisensory marketing is often limited to the two most dominant senses: sight and sound. While multisensory XR technology can include olfactory and haptic (sense of touch) stimuli, it is not yet mainstream.

Therefore, in Marketing 6.0, blending the digital and multisensory experiences is crucial, particularly when digital fatigue sets in as customers spend hours interacting with digital devices and receiving vast amounts of content daily. Combining physical and digital experiences can create a more memorable and engaging customer experience beyond what is possible with just one medium.

The second type is spatial marketing experience. Spatial marketing is revolutionizing how businesses interact with customers by seamlessly integrating physical objects with human behavior. By leveraging technology and design, companies can create a more immersive experience for their customers. Imagine a retail store where video ads play as you walk by or a restaurant where the lighting and ambiance change based on the time of day. With spatial marketing, businesses can automate machines to synchronize with human movements and provide personalized experiences that leave a lasting impression on their customers.

Amazon has been a leader in implementing this type of customer experience. Its Amazon Go chain of physical stores utilizes advanced technologies, which allow customers to enter the store, pick up the items they want, and leave without having to check out or interact with a cashier. Instead, customers are charged for the items via their Amazon account, which is automatically charged upon exit. This frictionless shopping experience is called "Just Walk Out" and is implemented at Whole Foods Market and other Amazon Web Services (AWS) clients.

Lastly, the most experimental type is the metaverse marketing experience. Marketing in the metaverse is a relatively new concept, with 2021 being seen as the beginning of its emergence. Metaverses exist primarily as gaming or entertainment platforms, leading many brands to explore in-game advertising in their overall media strategy. Global brands such as Nike, Coca-Cola, and Samsung are early adopters, offering digital collectibles and digital engagement in currently available metaverses.

Marketing in the metaverses might seem implausible for most older generations. But it feels second nature for Generation Z and Generation Alpha, born and raised when the boundary between traditional and digital realms has dissolved. Generation Z and Generation Alpha are digital natives. They are accustomed to digital interactions and immersive multiscreen environments. Generation Alpha may even be considered AI and Metaverse natives, growing up in the age of virtual assistants, personalized social feeds, and virtual-world-building games.

Summary: From Multi to Omni to Meta

Marketing has evolved to address global challenges and changing customer expectations. Incorporating sustainability themes and new technologies for customer engagement are essential for businesses to remain relevant.

Indeed, marketing has shifted from traditional to digital, but most customers still value some forms of human interaction. As a result, multichannel and omnichannel marketing have become popular among marketers aiming to leverage both traditional and digital engagement.

Metamarketing goes beyond that and offers a genuine physical and digital convergence by providing a more interactive and immersive customer experience across physical and digital spaces. Metamarketing is increasingly important in engaging Generation Z and Generation Alpha, so organizations need to begin embracing it.

REFLECTION QUESTIONS

- Are you ready to move from omnichannel marketing to metamarketing? Explore the potential obstacles that might prevent you from creating a more interactive and immersive experience.

- Observe Generation Z and Generation Alpha around you and the technologies they use daily. Think about why they are spending so much time in virtual worlds. Then, explore the best way to engage with them as your main markets in the next decades.

CHAPTER 2

The Emergence of Phygital Natives

Young Generation Z and Generation Alpha Coming of Age

In the last decade, marketers have favored Generation Y, or the millennials, as a focus audience due to their sheer size and high purchasing power. Consequently, marketers have adjusted their strategies to adapt to Generation Y's key characteristics, such as a strong focus on sustainability and tech savviness.

Modern marketers have created more campaigns highlighting eco-friendly products or socially responsible operations. For example, fashion brands such as Patagonia and Everlane have tapped into the millennial mindset by focusing on recycled and sustainably produced materials and becoming the antithesis of the fast fashion industry.

Marketers have also leveraged digital marketing tactics such as social media and search engine marketing to reach Generation Y. Even luxury fashion groups such as LVMH and Kering, traditionally known for investing heavily in offline experiences, have shifted half of their marketing budget to digital media. This shift toward digital marketing has allowed these brands to reach a wider audience of millennials.

Marketing strategies have evolved to become more sustainable, digital, and social to cater to the increasing influence of millennials. However, it does not stop there, as marketers are expanding their efforts to engage with even younger generations: Generation Z and Generation Alpha.

Embracing Phygital Natives

Today, marketers increasingly focus on Generation Z and Generation Alpha, true *digital natives* who grew up with the mainstream Internet. Generation Z, born between the mid-1990s to early 2010s, was born into the digital age and is highly adaptable to new technologies. Generation Alpha, the following cohort born after 2010, is expected to be even more digitally savvy due to growing up with millennial parents who are also tech-savvy. Together, they account for more than four billion people globally, making them a key market for brands.

Although they share some similarities with Generation Y in digital savviness, some differences set Generation Z and Generation Alpha apart (see Figure 2.1). Generation Y, experiencing the Internet later in life, often views it as a mere tool. In contrast, Generation Z and Generation Alpha, who have grown up with the Internet as a constant presence, consider it an integral part of their daily experience. They are connected continuously through multiple screens, even in social situations. As a result, these younger cohorts have a higher level of immersion in digital environments. Marketers, therefore, have to rethink ways to engage with them.

Due to a lifetime of immersion in digital stimulation and massive messages targeted their way, Generation Z and Generation Alpha have selective attention spans. It has resulted in a preference for personalized content and a tendency to ignore irrelevant messages. They also skip longer advertisements and prefer short-form content, memes, and emoji.

Yet they can spend hours binging on Netflix and be deeply absorbed in playing online games with their friends. It suggests they have no problem sustaining their attention span when the content is highly engaging and personalized to their interests.

TikTok's rise exemplifies this. The popularity of its short-form format and robust personalization algorithm among Generation Z prompted Instagram and YouTube to follow

THE DIFFERENT PROFILE OF GEN Z AND GEN ALPHA

GEN Y

DIGITAL SAVVY

Grew up with the Internet during teenage years and young adulthood

Internet as a tool

Separation between online and offline activities

Idealistic and conformist

Prioritizing material possesions

GEN Z AND GEN ALPHA

DIGITAL NATIVE

Born into a world where the Internet is ubiquitous

Internet as an integral part of life

No separation between online and offline activities

Pragmatic and nonconformist

Prioritizing experiences

FIGURE 2.1   The Generational Difference.

suit with their versions called Reels and Shorts, respectively. These new platforms accommodate selective attention, allowing them to scroll short-form content endlessly on social media. The preference for brief, visual content also extends to Internet search behavior, with Generation Z favoring platforms such as YouTube, Instagram, and TikTok over traditional browsing on Google.

We could argue that this strong preference for hyper-personalized content means that Generation Z and Generation Alpha are *artificial intelligence (AI) natives*. While they do not necessarily understand AI technology more than other generations, they grew up seeing the value of sharing their data in exchange for more contextual and personalized experiences.

Moreover, they are comfortable interacting with AI-powered voice assistants such as Apple's Siri or Amazon's Alexa to make their lives more convenient. Students and young professionals are beginning to actively use ChatGPT or similar language models to help with school and office work. Some even prefer chatbots to human customer service representatives to handle quick inquiries and complaints.

Generation Z and Generation Alpha are also *metaverse natives*. Their love for online gaming suggests they are comfortable with immersive digital environments and virtual communities. Gaming is popular for these generations, who are drawn to the highly immersive digital content, engaging competition with peers, and tightly knit online communities that gaming offers.

While Generation Y like to gather in person when gaming, Generation Z and Generation Alpha tend to connect remotely in virtual gaming environments. The younger cohorts are also more likely to spend money buying in-game items to enhance their avatars and improve their gaming experience. In addition, they are comfortable interacting with user interfaces that use augmented reality (AR) and virtual reality (VR) technologies.

Nevertheless, engaging younger generations does not necessarily mean focusing solely on online experiences. In fact, recent research shows that Generation Z, despite being known as digital natives, still enjoys shopping in physical stores. A McKinsey survey across 25 product categories reveals that, although Generation Z in the United States makes many online purchases, they are also more likely to shop in physical stores than Generation Y.

Likewise, research by A.S. Watson—the world's largest health and beauty retail group—shows that Generation Z prefers offline shopping for beauty products, citing physical stores' social interactions and experiential aspects as key attractions. Moreover, Generation Z also seeks technology-enhanced physical stores and online-offline integrated apps for a more immersive and seamless shopping experience.

The reason for this seemingly paradoxical insight is simple. Being digital natives, Generation Z and Generation Alpha see no border between the physical and digital worlds in their daily lives. For instance, they can shop in stores while checking prices on their smartphone—seamlessly switching from offline to online. They can also fluidly start a conversation in person and continue the discussion on messaging apps or watch concerts while sharing their experiences on social media. The phenomenon is known as *phygital*—a hybrid of physical and digital.

Despite their young age, Generation Z and Generation Alpha represent a sophisticated customer base that demands an advanced marketing approach. Generation Z and Generation Alpha truly embrace interactive and immersive customer experiences, online and offline. They are

GEN Z AND GEN ALPHA ARE PHYGITAL NATIVES

Connect continuously through
multiple screens, even in social
situations

GEN Z AND GEN ALPHA

see no border between the
physical and digital worlds in their
daily lives

Understand the value of AI for
contextual and personalized
experiences

Comfortable with immersive
environments and virtual
communities

FIGURE 2.2 The Phygital Natives.

what we call the *phygital natives* (see Figure 2.2). Therefore, marketers need to adopt next-generation digital technologies to engage with them effectively without neglecting the traditional physical touchpoints.

Phygital Natives Getting Older Younger

The sophistication of the younger cohorts can be attributed to their accelerated maturity. The phenomenon of *kids getting older younger* (KGOY) is increasingly apparent as younger generations adopt behaviors and preferences usually associated with older age groups.

This includes teenagers dressing up, wearing makeup, engaging in mature conversations, and entering romantic relationships earlier than previous generations. Furthermore, children start using technology products, such as smartphones and tablets, and consuming mature content across media platforms at a younger age. But the faster maturity goes beyond emulating the looks and purchases of older generations.

People typically go through four life stages: *fundamental*, *forefront*, *fostering*, and *final*—each takes approximately 20 years:

- The *fundamental* stage focuses on learning and identity formation through education and social relationships.
- The *forefront* stage involves transitioning from learning to work, taking risks, and exploring life while building a career and engaging in romantic relationships.
- The *fostering* stage is characterized by settling down, building a family, nurturing others, and contributing to society.
- Lastly, the *final* stage revolves around adapting to old age, managing health and relationships, enjoying meaningful activities, and imparting wisdom to younger generations.

Generation Z and Generation Alpha experience accelerated life stages, adopting mature mindsets at younger ages. They demonstrate a greater willingness to take risks and learn through hands-on experiences, effectively going through the *fundamental* and *forefront* steps simultaneously in their development. Usually appearing during the *fostering* stage, the desire to contribute to society and achieve work-life balance is already present in many Generation Z in their mid-20s.

This KGOY trend stems from multiple factors. Firstly, younger generations have easier access to information through the Internet and its digital content. Moreover, brands targeting younger audiences in areas such as fashion, food and beverages, consumer electronics, and beauty are introducing them to these product categories at an earlier age.

Parenting style also has a significant impact on their behavior. For instance, parents from Generation X and Generation Y often encourage their children—belonging to Generation Z and Generation Alpha—to take on more adult responsibilities at home. All these factors lead to younger generations' faster mental and emotional growth.

Characteristics of Phygital Natives

The KGOY phenomenon has significant implications for the characteristics of Generation Z and Generation Alpha. These younger generations are highly pragmatic and thoroughly research information on the Internet before making decisions. They prioritize authenticity and are attracted to

THE UNIQUENESS OF GEN Z AND GEN ALPHA

ARE HIGHLY PRAGMATIC

VALUE AUTHENTICITY

GEN Z AND GEN ALPHA

SEEK SELF-EXPRESSION AT A YOUNGER AGE

FIGURE 2.3 The Characteristics of Phygital Natives.

brands whose values align with their own. Additionally, they seek self-actualization at a younger age and invest time in building their persona online (see Figure 2.3). By understanding these mature psychographic and behavioral profiles, marketers can position their brands better in the mind of younger generations.

Pragmatic Attitude and Decision Making

Generation Z grew up during the Great Recession (2007–2009) and witnessed their parents and older siblings' financial struggles. It leads to heightened financial awareness compared to Generation Y. Thus, they are interested in learning about personal finance, saving money, and investing for the future.

This caution is also evident in the workplace. Generation Z workforce is more realistic compared to their idealistic Generation Y counterparts. They tend to prioritize job security over pursuing their dream job or high salaries, particularly considering the looming recession and widespread layoffs. As reported by Glassdoor, younger workers are increasingly drawn to larger, well-established companies, in contrast to millennials, who are often attracted to trendy start-ups.

Generation Z is also more adept at making informed decisions and evaluating products and services from online and offline sources. As a result, they are sensible and understand value well—focusing on price and quality rather than solely relying on brand names. In terms of value, they put more weight on functional benefits than emotional appeal.

Unlike Generation Y, which tends to spend more on materialistic products, Generation Z and Generation Alpha spend more on experiences such as traveling, gaming, wellness activities, live events and concerts, and community engagements.

Rather than valuing possessions, these younger generations are more inclined to invest in themselves, placing greater importance on personal growth gained from experiences. This preference aligns well with the sharing economy, allowing them to access goods and services without the need for ownership through the likes of Uber and Airbnb.

This value orientation also poses significant challenges for established and heritage brands relying on reputation and history to attract customers. The younger generations are less likely to be swayed by brand recognition and are more likely to seek novelty and new experiences that meet their specific needs. As a result, brands need to innovate customer experience to remain relevant.

Marketers must consider their pragmatic nature when crafting customer experiences for younger generations. Convenience takes precedence over flashy features and needless touchpoints. Even immersive, high-tech interactions should be purposeful and practical. Metaverse experiences requiring costly devices and additional steps may not resonate with these young consumers.

Authenticity and Relationship with Brands

The pragmatic nature of younger generations influences their connections with brands. In contrast to the more conformist Generation Y, who often succumb to peer pressure to fit in, Generation Z and Generation Alpha gravitate toward brands that align with their values.

For instance, Generation Z and Generation Alpha are more likely to support brands that demonstrate environmental responsibility and ethical practices. Examples of such brands include TOMS Shoes, which donates a pair of shoes for every pair sold. For them, consumption is closely linked to sustainability.

As the most racially and ethnically diverse generations in US history, Generation Z and Generation Alpha are incredibly inclusive, making friends online and offline. They love harmony and synergy with those around them—family, friends, coworkers, and communities. At work, Generation Z tends to avoid confrontations, prefer dialogues, and accept differences in viewpoints.

These generations also value brands championing diversity, equity, and inclusion (DEI) in their corporate culture. In the workplace, it has become essential for employers to adhere to these values to attract and retain these younger employees.

For example, Microsoft has implemented initiatives to increase the representation of women and minorities in the tech industry. Other prominent companies, such as Johnson & Johnson and Procter & Gamble, are also recognized for their commitments to DEI.

The youth also calls on the brands to keep it real. Generation Z recognizes and rejects the portrayal of unrealistic perfection in traditional advertising. Instead, they prefer brands that embrace imperfections. This preference can be seen in the beauty industry, for example, where there is a shift in spending from cosmetics to skincare and natural look, as reported by Kantar.

The trend is evident in the realm of social media as well. Generation Y prefers aspirational and professionally made content, whereas Generation Z and Generation Alpha audiences tend to resonate more with raw, unfiltered content on platforms such as TikTok and Instagram. The younger cohorts want to see unscripted moments in real-life scenarios instead of staged content. User-generated content (UGC) is a powerful way for brands to tap into this desire for authenticity.

Individual Expression and Digital Persona

The younger generations aspire to the same level of individual authenticity they demand from companies. Despite the pressure to conform that comes with social media, Generation Z and Generation Alpha are embracing individuality and self-expression. They personify diversity not only in the real world but also in the digital realm.

Many youngsters dedicate several hours daily to creating distinctive digital identities through their smartphones, computers, and even gaming consoles. On platforms such as TikTok and Instagram, users showcase their individuality through profile pictures, posts, and accounts they follow. Some even use pseudonyms and pay for personalized avatars on games such as Fortnite and Minecraft to further enhance their online persona.

The Dolly Parton Challenge, a viral social media meme in 2020, illustrates people's efforts to build digital imagery. The challenge asks people to share four photos, each representing their images on LinkedIn, Facebook, Instagram, and Tinder. This challenge has been embraced by both individuals and brands, demonstrating how they adapt their appearance to fit different social media platforms.

Observations suggest that Generation Y presents a very different persona for each type of social media channel, reflecting the tendency to use specific social media platforms for different audiences and objectives. In contrast, Generation Z uses more uniform images to create consistent and less platform-dependent imagery.

The trend of maintaining a consistent online identity is driving newer social media platforms to broaden their capabilities and become multipurpose. One example is Tik-Tok, which started as an entertainment-focused platform but has since expanded to include live-streaming commerce, job discovery through features such as TikTok Resumes, and even serving as an alternative search engine for Generation Z.

Younger generations are also increasingly adopting community-based social media platforms such as Reddit, Discord, and Twitch, alongside feed-based ones such as TikTok, Instagram, and Twitter. Indeed, community-based platforms often offer better anonymity and data privacy, a growing concern for younger users.

But these platforms are popular among younger generations because they cater to niche interests and subcultures, providing a more personalized online experience. Most importantly, these platforms provide opportunities for interactive experiences. They tend to have more engaged and active communities, allowing users to connect with like-minded individuals.

Summary: Young Generation Z and Generation Alpha Coming of Age

Modern marketers have adapted their strategies to cater to millennials, focusing on sustainability and digital marketing tactics. Now, marketers should shift their attention to younger generations, Generation Z and Generation Alpha, digital natives who prefer interactive and immersive experiences, both online and offline.

Generation Z and Generation Alpha are experiencing accelerated maturity, adopting mature mindsets and behaviors faster than previous generations. They are highly pragmatic, value authenticity, and seek self-expression at a younger age, making it essential for marketers to understand these profiles to position their brands better.

REFLECTION QUESTIONS

- How can you balance the demand for hyper-personalized digital experiences with the desire for physical touchpoints among Generation Z and Generation Alpha, who are increasingly becoming *phygital*?
- With younger generations experiencing accelerated maturity, how can brands effectively communicate values and engage with these cohorts while remaining true to their brand positioning?

CHAPTER 3

The Inevitability of Immersive Marketing

Five Micro-Trends Leading to Metamarketing

As digital lifestyles have become an integral part of the lives of Generation Z and Generation Alpha, businesses need to adapt to stay relevant. Fundamental shifts have developed in several components of marketing in a digital world.

There are five essential components to marketing in a digital world, the first being *content*. Content refers to information created, consumed, and shared across digital media. It can take the form of written materials such as short messages, press releases, articles, newsletters, whitepapers, case studies, and even books. It can also be more visual, such as images, infographics, comics, interactive graphics, presentation slides, games, videos, short films, and even feature films.

The second component is *social media*, which has become the primary channel for distributing and amplifying content. According to a Morning Consult survey in 2022, 98 percent of Generation Z in the United States used social media, and 71 percent used it for three hours or more daily. Generation Z's five most popular social media are YouTube, Instagram, TikTok, Snapchat, and Facebook.

While social media is mainly a communication channel, the third component, *e-commerce*, is a sales channel. The US e-commerce market is the second largest in the world after China. According to the US Census Bureau, the estimated e-commerce sales in 2022 exceeded $1 trillion, accounting for 14.6 percent of total sales in the United States. The major players in US e-commerce include the online marketplace Amazon, online auction site eBay, and offline-to-online (O2O) store Walmart.com.

The next two components are fundamental enablers of marketing in a digital world. *Artificial intelligence* (AI), the fourth component, plays a vital role behind the scene. For example, AI ensures that content reaches its intended audience on social media. AI analyzes user behavior and interests and delivers personalized content to specific user segments. Similarly, AI also works behind any e-commerce platform providing users with suitable product recommendations.

FIGURE 3.1   Five Microtrends Leading to Metamarketing.

The fifth and final component is *devices*, with the smartphone being the most important. Smartphones and other devices, such as tablets and laptops, provide access to social media content and e-commerce applications. Pew Research Center estimated that 85 percent of Americans own a smartphone, while approximately half own a tablet. With a vast array of apps available to download on these devices, users can do various digital activities.

Across these five components, we have observed several subtle and not-so-obvious shifts. Each of these micro-trends signals a major marketing movement toward a more interactive and immersive approach (see Figure 3.1).

Short-Form Video Content

Due to the widespread use of mobile devices in our daily routines, there has been a significant change in how people consume media. Instead of fixed, prolonged online sessions, people have hundreds of brief sessions throughout the day. During these sessions, people experience impulsive moments where they choose to learn, do, discover, or purchase products. These split-second decision-making opportunities are called micro-moments by Google and Boston Consulting Group.

Customers may pull out their phones and consume content on social media during micro-moments, which can occur while commuting on the subway or waiting in line at the store. In these moments, brands must be present and engage potential customers by providing relevant information and assistance that meet their needs.

Given the narrow window of opportunity, short-form content is ideal for micro-moments. Moreover, the bite-sized content matches Generation Z and Generation Alpha's selective attention spans, providing a quick and easy way to consume information on mobile phones. In addition, the short format allows brands and content creators to produce content quickly and adapt to fast-changing trends. That is why we see more short-form content in social media today.

While short-form content can take many formats, such as articles, images, or infographics, video content remains the most favored. Video content can quickly capture the audience's attention and convey complex messages effectively. Additionally, video content can be highly engaging, making it more shareable. With content creation and editing tools available on social media such as TikTok, Instagram, and YouTube, it is easier than ever to produce video content quickly.

Short-form video content should be shoppable to be fully effective during micro-moments, allowing consumers to purchase directly from the content. Shoppable content typically includes links or tags that enable consumers to buy the featured product or service without leaving social media. It triggers consumers to act impulsively after consuming the content, making it an effective tool for brands looking to capitalize on the audience's interest at the moment of discovery.

For example, Target utilizes Instagram videos to inspire potential customers during micro-moments by showcasing new clothing collections, offering home decoration ideas,

SHORT-FORM VIDEOS FOR MICRO-MOMENTS

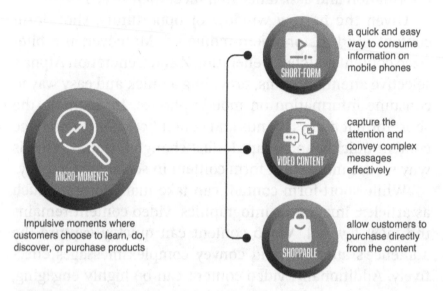

MICRO-MOMENTS

Impulsive moments where customers choose to learn, do, discover, or purchase products

SHORT-FORM
a quick and easy way to consume information on mobile phones

VIDEO CONTENT
capture the attention and convey complex messages effectively

SHOPPABLE
allow customers to purchase directly from the content

FIGURE 3.2 Short-Form Video Content.

and sharing recipes. By including links to the featured products in the videos, Target can drive more sales conversions.

In conclusion, micro-moments are characterized by customers fully immersing themselves in digital content with a decision-making mindset. Brands can take advantage of these moments by creating short-form videos that entertain the audience while providing relevant information and inspiration (see Figure 3.2).

Community-Based Social Media

The social media landscape has appeared relatively static in recent years, with big players such as Facebook, YouTube, Instagram, and TikTok still dominating the space with at least one billion monthly users. However, there have been some subtle shifts below the surface as relatively smaller platforms such as Reddit, Discord, and Mastodon gain momentum. This trend does not necessarily indicate that users will abandon major platforms altogether. Instead, they will likely allocate social media time to these smaller ones.

One key reason for this trend is the growing anxiety and concern over data privacy when posting or sharing content on large platforms. As a result, social media users increasingly seek to engage with several smaller communities they trust and with whom they share the same interests. These users seek social platforms that balance public and private spaces to have more control over their digital lives.

One example of a community-based social media platform is Reddit. It is a platform for sharing and discussing content within dedicated communities organized around specific interests such as gaming, sports, and business. In Reddit, users can post content, and other users can then vote and comment on these posts, leading to a ranking system determining which posts are the most visible.

Another community-based social media platform is Discord, which hosts real-time text, voice, and video chats. Initially popular only among gamers, Discord allows users within a server to communicate and share content. With 150 million monthly active users, Discord is hardly a small platform. However, while other social media functions as big public spaces, Discord is organized into discrete communities called "servers." This trend of community-based servers has prompted WhatsApp to introduce similar features called "communities," which serve as a more extensive umbrella to already popular but smaller WhatsApp groups.

The most distinctive community-based social platform, however, is Mastodon. It is a microblogging platform similar to Twitter, where users can post short messages known as "toots" instead of "tweets." But the major difference is that Mastodon is a decentralized, open-source social platform that is community-run, which means no specific company owns it. Instead of being hosted on a centralized server like Twitter, Mastodon comprises many individual servers, called "instances," focusing on particular interests.

The rise of community-based social media such as Reddit, Discord, and Mastodon indicates that users are looking for platforms built around real connection and deep conversation (see Figure 3.3). Moreover, it coincides with the rise

THE RISE OF COMMUNAL SOCIAL MEDIA

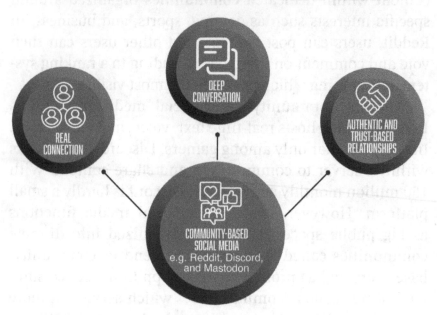

FIGURE 3.3 Community-Based Social Media.

of Generation Z and Generation Alpha, who seek authentic and trust-based relationships. Therefore, they do not want the content they consume on social media governed by platform algorithms. Instead, they prefer to let the trusted community decide what they see.

Interactive E-Commerce

E-commerce, which involves buying and selling products and services online, has significantly evolved in recent years. Typically, e-commerce transactions occur through online platforms such as direct-to-consumer websites or intermediary marketplaces. For example, Nike sells its products directly through its e-commerce website and various marketplaces such as Amazon and Zappos. However, there are now additional e-commerce models available to businesses.

A rapidly growing trend is social commerce, in which transactions occur on social media. Businesses can turn their social media pages into shoppable storefronts by creating content that prompts users to purchase and facilitating transactions within the social media platforms. To enable this seamless browsing and buying experience, social media platforms such as Facebook, Instagram, TikTok, and Pinterest have integrated shopping features such as product catalogs, shopping carts, and payment systems.

Another emerging e-commerce model that is gaining popularity is conversational commerce. This approach involves transactions directly within messaging apps such as WhatsApp and Meta's Messenger. It enables buyers to ask questions and receive real-time seller responses, increasing the likelihood of a purchase. Conversational commerce can be conducted with human agents or through automated chatbots. Combining both allows businesses to offer customers 24/7 support and personalized responses, which can help companies to build stronger relationships with their customers.

Lastly, the newest e-commerce model transforming online shopping is livestream commerce, which has become increasingly popular in China and is now gaining traction in the United States. This approach involves sellers promoting and selling products through live video broadcasts, similar to TV home shopping on QVC. However, in livestream commerce, the interaction is much greater as buyers can engage with sellers via chat or reaction buttons and even purchase the products in real time.

Today, all the major platforms in the United States—Amazon, Facebook, YouTube, and TikTok—offer livestream commerce. In addition, retailers such as Walmart and Nordstrom and TV networks such as QVC and HSN are also adopting this approach.

Social commerce, conversational commerce, and livestream commerce are popular with Generation Z, and the sales through these models will reach $107 billion by 2025, as projected by eMarketer. But more importantly, the emergence of these models highlights the growing significance of engaging content and real-time interactions in e-commerce (see Figure 3.4). Customers today seek ways to engage with brands and businesses during product discovery, as it helps them make more informed decisions. As a result, companies prioritizing interactive customer experiences, which metamarketing offers, are likely to have a competitive advantage in the e-commerce market.

NEW FORMS OF E-COMMERCE

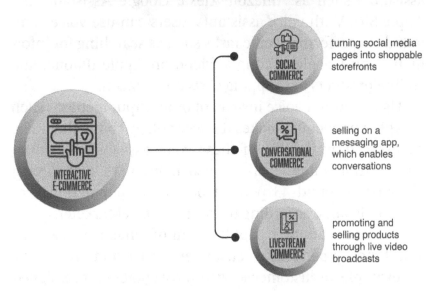

FIGURE 3.4 Interactive E-Commerce.

Language-Based AI

In a nutshell, AI uses computer algorithms to perform tasks that usually require human intelligence. One exciting development in AI is natural language processing (NLP), which trains machines to replicate the human way of communication, in both written and spoken forms.

NLP is a fundamental component of language-based AI that can understand and generate human language. Language-based AI comprehends users' questions and can respond according to its knowledge repository. In a way, it acts as a conversation partner, enabling humans to interact with computers to access information. Examples of language-based AI enabling two-way communications include voice assistants, chatbots, and ChatGPT.

A common use of language-based AI is for voice assistants such as Amazon Alexa, Google Assistant, and Apple Siri. With voice assistants, users can use voice commands to perform specific tasks such as searching for information on Google, texting a friend on Apple iPhone, and adding products to shopping carts on Amazon.

Using natural voice instead of other input methods such as typing or clicking makes the technology compelling. The widespread availability of these voice assistants in smartphones and home speakers also helps with mainstream adoption. Around 43 percent of the US population uses voice assistants, according to estimates by eMarketer.

Chatbot is another popular form of language-based AI, found mostly performing customer service and sales tasks. For example, in customer service, most chatbots are assigned to respond to inquiries according to a preprogrammed script. Chatbots can also be trained to nurture sales leads by providing relevant information on products and services. Apart from delivering a streamlined customer experience, chatbots also bring cost efficiency to brands.

For basic inquiries, most customers (74 percent) still favor using chatbots, according to PSFK research. Therefore, leading brands such as Starbucks, Spotify, and Sephora use chatbots for customer interactions. With these chatbots, customers can easily order coffee, get music recommendations, and obtain shopping assistance.

A chatbot rising in popularity is OpenAI's ChatGPT—the fastest technology product to hit a milestone of 100 million users. In comparison, it took nine months for TikTok and two and a half years for Instagram to acquire the same user base, according to UBS analysis based on Sensor Tower data. Indeed, technology adoption is accelerating. Today's customers do not hesitate to adopt new technologies that bring convenience and improve their lives.

What makes ChatGPT different from other chatbots is that it is highly contextual, with the ability to understand not only the content users are saying but also the context of the user's intent and sentiment. Furthermore, ChatGPT has proven excellent at generating complex and coherent texts. Businesses, for example, can use ChatGPT to draft personalized advertising copy, summarize lengthy reports, and analyze massive customer data.

AI and NLP have a long history, with early development dating back to the 1950s. But in recent years, the technologies have become widely used with the rising popularity of voice assistants, chatbots, and ChatGPT, as well as the emergence of Generation Z (see Figure 3.5). This development in the human-machine interface is paving the way for the more interactive metamarketing.

FORMS OF LANGUAGE-BASED ARTIFICIAL INTELLIGENCE

VOICE ASSISTANT

CHATBOT

LARGE LANGUAGE MODEL

Use voice commands to perform specific tasks, e.g. Amazon Alexa, Google Assistant, and Apple Siri

Get quick responses to basic inquiries according to a preprogrammed script

Generate complex and coherent texts with prompts, e.g. OpenAI's ChatGPT

FIGURE 3.5   Language-Based Artificial Intelligence.

Immersive Wearable Devices

Consumer electronics companies are increasingly venturing into immersive devices. Immersive devices are any form of technology that enables users to experience digital content in a way that creates a sense of being surrounded by it.

Two examples of immersive tech are augmented reality (AR) and virtual reality (VR). AR overlays digital content onto the real world, allowing users to interact with the real and virtual elements simultaneously. An example of augmented reality would be using your smartphone's camera to view your surroundings and seeing digital images, such as a Pokémon, overlaid onto the real world.

On the other hand, VR immerses the user in a completely digital environment, creating an experience separate from the physical world. An example of virtual reality would be using a VR headset to enter a completely digital world, such as a simulated game, where the user can interact with virtual objects and characters as if they were there.

Immersive devices are often bulky and expensive, limiting their availability to a small group of professional users. For example, VR headsets such as the Oculus Rift and HTC Vive require powerful computers and are uncomfortable for extended use.

However, a trend has emerged toward making immersive technology devices more wearable and accessible for most people. Currently available wearables that offer immersive experiences include three-dimensional (3D) audio earbuds and smart glasses.

Immersive 3D audio is a technology that creates the illusion of sound surrounding the listener, simulating how sound is heard in the real world. For example, listening to music on 3D audio will make users feel that they are listening to live music, where different instruments and vocals are coming from different directions and distances. Some examples of 3D audio are Apple's *Spatial Audio* and Sony's *360 Reality,* which are available in the earbuds the brands produce.

Another trending wearable is smart glasses such as Ray-Ban Stories, which have audio features to answer calls or listen to music and a camera to take pictures and videos. Some, including Amazon Echo Frames and Razer Anzu, are compatible with voice assistants, allowing users to use voice commands to operate the glasses. More advanced glasses have AR capabilities with built-in displays, which project information in the wearer's field of view. This information may include videos, messages, and navigation directions.

These immersive wearables designed for consumers transform how people consume digital audio and video content by providing a more hands-free experience than smartphones while offering the same functionalities and accessibility. Unlike smartphones, wearables enable people to interact with their surrounding environment while accessing digital content, making the whole experience more immersive (see Figure 3.6).

EMERGING IMMERSIVE WEARABLES

VIDEO REALITY HEADSETS
Head-mounted displays for virtual reality uses, e.g. Oculus Rift

3D AUDIO EARBUDS
Earbuds that create 3D sound illusion, e.g. Apple's AirPods with Spatial Audio

SMART GLASSES
Glasses with audio, display, and camera features, e.g. Ray-Ban Stories

FIGURE 3.6   Immersive Wearable Devices.

Summary: Five Micro-Trends Leading to Metamarketing

We are seeing the rise of micro-trends in five key areas of the digital lifestyle—content, social media, e-commerce, AI, and devices—that reflect younger generations' preference for more interactive and immersive experiences. Short-form video is becoming prevalent to tap into immersive micro-moments during the customer journey, while social media is shifting toward smaller, more specialized communities. In addition, e-commerce is expanding beyond traditional websites and marketplaces to include more interactive models such as social commerce, conversational commerce, and livestream commerce.

On the software side, language-based AI, such as voice assistants, chatbots, and ChatGPT, enables seamless human-machine interaction critical for interactive marketing. Finally, on the hardware side, consumer electronics companies are creating affordable wearable devices to provide immersive digital experiences.

REFLECTION QUESTIONS

- How do you think the rise of community-based platforms will impact the dominance of more prominent social media such as Facebook and Instagram? Will the smaller platforms eventually get bigger, or will the larger ones adapt to the community-based trend?

- How do you think immersive technology devices will transform how audiences consume digital content in the future? What are some potential challenges for making them more mainstream?

CHAPTER 4

The Future of Customer Experience

Fusing Physical and Digital for Complete Immersion

There is a growing trend among marketers to redirect their focus from creating and selling products to delivering exceptional customer experience. This shift has broadened the marketing scope from a single function to a cross-functional approach, as the customer experience encompasses all interactions and points of contact a customer has with a company.

It may include various touchpoints such as exposure to advertising, searching on Google, browsing the aisle, using the product, making warranty claims, and discussing the product on social media. The impact of each touchpoint is influenced by the context of other touchpoints, making the customer experience holistic and integrated. Therefore, customer experience is a multifaceted concept greater than the sum of its parts.

The movement toward competing in the realm of customer experience can be attributed to several factors. First, transparency on the Internet can lead to the faster commoditization of products, as customers and competitors can easily compare product specifications. It enables customers to make well-informed choices and competitors to emulate the top products in the market quickly.

Companies must now rely more on intangible factors to differentiate their products as the gap between tangible features diminishes. Creating and launching a new product alone is not enough. The customer experience with a product, from discovery to purchase and usage, has become equally important as the product itself. Unlike product specifications, customer experience is subjective, with each customer having a unique and personal experience, making it less susceptible to commoditization.

Another reason customer experience has become a winning marketing strategy is the shortened product life cycle. Social media causes rapid shifts in younger generations' product preferences, leading to a shorter life cycle. Social media often determines what is trendy and desirable. With products becoming less popular quickly, companies have a narrower window to generate revenue from them, which has led to the need to launch new products frequently. This can be a challenging task. Nevertheless, providing a unique customer experience can prolong the product life cycle.

Marketers are forced to innovate on customer experience due to accelerated commoditization and shortened product life cycles. However, improving customer experience not only addresses these challenges but also leads to increased revenue (see Figure 4.1). Elevating the customer experience leads to greater engagement, as customers spend more time with products, resulting in a greater likelihood for them to have a higher willingness to pay, buy more of the same products, and share their experiences with their friends and family.

Coca-Cola, a global heritage brand, serves as a prime example. While the flagship product has been unchanged for over 130 years, Coca-Cola continuously reinvents the customer experience of buying and consuming the product to maintain relevance among younger generations.

The campaigns have always tapped into the latest trends. For instance, the worldwide "Share a Coke" campaign capitalized on the personalization trend among young generations by featuring 250 of the most popular names in each country on its bottles. In the "Friendly Twist" campaign, Coca-Cola introduced vending machines on campuses

FIGURE 4.1 The Customer Experience Imperative.

stocked with specially designed bottles that could only be opened when locked and twisted together with matching bottles. This innovative design encouraged social interaction, which is lacking due to addiction to mobile phones.

In recent years, Coca-Cola has been the pioneer in embracing the immersive experience trend. It introduced Coca-Cola Creations, a range of limited-edition beverages that reimagined the iconic Coca-Cola taste, complemented by immersive experiences across physical and digital realms.

One variant in this line is Coca-Cola Starlight, which envisions how outer space might taste. By scanning a can or bottle of this new flavor via the Coca-Cola Creations website, users can access an augmented-reality concert featuring US singer and brand ambassador Ava Max. Another variant is Coca-Cola Zero Sugar Byte, a gaming-inspired drink that imagines what pixels taste like and comes with immersive experiences. Coca-Cola created a virtual island in the online video game Fortnite that showcases the product alongside a mini-game collection.

Coca-Cola's marketing approach shows that the company understands the value of competing in the area of customer experience. Even when introducing new products, the company always strives to provide unique and trendy experiences integrated with the products.

The Future Is Immersive

Coca-Cola's recent marketing approach has demonstrated that the immersive customer experience is an imminent trend shaping modern marketing. The one-way broadcast campaign is no longer effective in capturing the audience's attention amid the overwhelming Internet and other media content. Immersive experiences are more engaging since they involve the customer physically or virtually as an integral part of the experience. Consider the difference between watching a concert on YouTube versus attending it live or studying from a book versus learning in a classroom.

For a customer experience to be immersive, every touchpoint has to be meticulously coordinated to deliver an encapsulated experience. Think of it as designing a live concert where every touchpoint contributes to the overall immersive customer experience.

In essence, five elements make up a complete immersion: multisensory, interactive, participative, frictionless, and storytelling experiences (see Figure 4.2). The multisensory experience stimulates the five senses (sight, sound, smell, taste, and touch) and better captures the audience's attention. In a concert, for example, these elements include stage design and visuals (sight), music performance and audio systems (sound), food and beverage (smell and taste), and physical contact among concertgoers (touch).

The interactive experience involves two-way dialogue, while the participative experience requires the customer to be actively involved. Some examples of interactions are pre-event meet and greets or audience engagement during the artist's performance, making the concert more memorable for participants.

In addition, the audience can actively participate by singing along, dancing, and clapping to the music, creating a more profound sense of immersion.

FIGURE 4.2   Five Elements of Immersive Experiences.

The frictionless experience facilitates the main attraction while minimizing any unnecessary obstacles. Examples of these peripheral touchpoints include buying tickets and merchandise and accessing the concert venue, all of which should be easy and hassle-free for the audience to focus on the main event.

Finally, the storytelling experience ties all the other elements into a cohesive narrative. An example of this can be seen in Bono's "Stories of Surrender" concert in 2022, where his music hits and monologues are interwoven with life stories from his memoir to create a flowing and meaningful narrative. When these five elements come together, they make a truly immersive experience.

Businesses can apply this same approach to create immersive experiences. The Apple Store is an excellent example of this. Even when customers can easily shop at apple.com, they still come to an Apple Store for the experience.

When you go to an Apple Store, you will see that the products are prominently displayed in an open space, inviting customers to try them out. Specifically, MacBooks are displayed with their screens tilted at 70 degrees, prompting customers to adjust the viewing angle and play with them, which creates a multisensory experience.

In the store, frontline staff will greet and assist you as you explore products. Apple trains its frontline workers to serve customers with an approach known as APPLE: *approaching* customers, *probing* to understand their needs, *presenting* solutions, actively *listening*, and *ending* the interaction with a farewell. Apple standardizes this interactive experience to ensure their employees serve with empathy.

The stores also offer a participative experience with "Today with Apple" sessions. In these series of hands-on classes and workshops, customers can learn various things such as iPhone photography, video editing, and music making.

With no cash registers or checkout lines, Apple's frontline staff can assist customers with payment anywhere in the store with their mobile devices and send the receipt via email. This is a frictionless experience that puts the product experience front and center.

Everything is then fused with famous Apple storytelling that focuses on simplicity and usability. In essence, Apple creates an innovative product that works with no fuss. Apple Stores are extensions of this company's product design principle in retail. Like Apple's products, the stores represent minimalism with their clean, uncluttered layout. Transactions and interactions are just intuitive for store visitors.

The Future Is Also Hybrid

Every immersive experience has physical and digital touchpoints that work seamlessly. Both types of touchpoints offer unique advantages that are rarely interchangeable. This is evident when comparing retail customer behavior during and after the COVID-19 pandemic. When physical distancing measures were still in place, customers turned to online shopping as a more convenient and safer option. As a result, e-commerce experienced rapid growth during this time.

However, as restrictions eased, many returned to physical outlets to shop. A survey conducted by Mood Media revealed that 71 percent of consumers worldwide now shop in physical stores as often or even more often than before the pandemic. As a result, many e-commerce players, such as Amazon and Shopify, have scaled back their operations as customers return to old habits, highlighting the benefits of brick-and-mortar shopping.

First, in-store shopping provides instant gratification since customers do not have to wait for goods to be delivered as when buying online. More importantly, it offers a range of multisensory experiences that allow customers to see, touch, and feel products. This hands-on experience often enhances customers' perception of the products and increases their desire to own them, making it more likely for a purchase to occur.

But the most important benefit of physical touchpoints— missing during the pandemic's e-commerce boom—is that they facilitate human-to-human interaction. Shopping is often a social experience that customers do with their friends and family, and they can also meet with frontline workers, building trust and long-term relationships.

While physical touchpoints offer these advantages, digital touchpoints still have their merits. Firstly, it is more efficient and flexible than in-store shopping since customers do not have to travel or spend time browsing through physical stores.

Moreover, online shopping offers a broader assortment of products, with access to trusted reviews, price comparisons, and deals, increasing customer confidence in purchasing decisions. Although customers cannot touch the products, they can still make informed choices based on the detailed information available.

Most importantly, online touchpoints allow for better personalization of products and promotions. Customers can receive recommendations based on their profile and history, making their experience more relevant.

With the rise of the *phygital native* who lives in both physical and digital spaces, incorporating digital touchpoints into the overall customer experience has become crucial for businesses. Although the post-pandemic trend suggests that most customer experiences in the next decade will occur primarily in physical spaces, companies need to incorporate digital touchpoints to some degree. The convenience, efficiency, and personalization of digital touchpoints can complement physical touchpoints and create a more immersive customer experience (see Figure 4.3).

COMBINING PHYSICAL AND DIGITAL EXPERIENCES

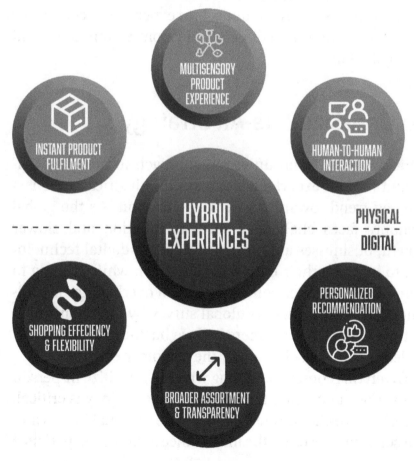

FIGURE 4.3   Merits of Online and Offline Experiences.

Metamarketing, the blending of physical and digital touchpoints into immersive experiences, is the key to winning the competition for customer experience. Digital touchpoints cater to customers who prioritize hassle-free and frictionless transaction experiences. While these touchpoints appeal to customers' rational and pragmatic sides, they will not completely replace physical experiences.

Customers seeking social interactions to fulfill their need for emotional and experiential connections prefer physical touchpoints. This implies that brick-and-mortar stores must evolve from just sales channels into experiential centers, or they will become indistinguishable from e-commerce and eventually fail.

No One-Size-Fits-All Strategy

Although there is no universal approach to merging digital and human experiences across all industries, there is a growing trend toward greater digitalization. As the global economy faces challenges such as inflation and slower growth, businesses are pressured to adopt digital technologies to improve their efficiency. However, while striving to increase digital touchpoints, they often overlook the significance of human touch. A global survey by PwC confirmed that two-thirds of customers believe businesses have disregarded the human element of the customer experience.

Given this context, knowing when to prioritize in-person interactions and when to incorporate technology is critical. Therefore, we classify customer experience touchpoints into four scenarios based on the importance of human experience in the overall customer experience and the extent to which digital experience can replace some touchpoints.

These scenarios exist within a spectrum. At one end of the spectrum (Scenario 1), the human touch is the least important, making full automation and frictionless experience possible. At the other end (Scenario 4), the human touch is of the utmost importance, making the augmented human-machine experience the best approach (see Figure 4.4). Understanding these four scenarios is essential in determining the best integration of digital technology and human touch.

Scenario 1: Human Presence Facilitates Transactions

There are certain scenarios where humans mainly serve as intermediaries for transactions, as in the case of bank tellers, supermarket cashiers, and ticket counters. The roles have well-defined procedures and are relatively straightforward. However, these roles have been increasingly replaced in recent years by digital touchpoints such as automated teller machines (ATMs), self-checkout machines, and self-service kiosks.

This shift toward digital touchpoints can be attributed to several factors, including the changing expectations of customers. Many customers prefer minimal social interaction in these transactional scenarios, as human connections are less relevant when the journey is relatively short. Instead, customers seek fast experiences that minimize friction and unnecessary contact.

COMBINING PHYSICAL AND DIGITAL EXPERIENCES

FIGURE 4.4 Replacing Human Experiences with Digital Experiences.

Furthermore, digital touchpoints make more business sense for companies. These routine transactions typically do not require sound judgment or a significant degree of personalization from frontline workers. Digital touchpoints can perform these transactions faster, more efficiently, and more accurately. Additionally, self-service digital touch-points are available 24/7, making them a preferable option for companies.

Digitalizing the human experience in this scenario is relatively straightforward since the goal is to remove friction. It will mainly involve implementing self-service and screen-based digital experiences with user-friendly user interfaces (UI) and user experiences (UX). For example, fast-food restaurants such as McDonald's, Taco Bell, and KFC have been introducing more self-service ordering kiosks in their locations. These kiosks have been reported to increase order amounts and margins, demonstrating the advantages of digital touchpoints.

Additionally, companies can use biometrics such as fingerprints, facial recognition, and other digital credentials to validate transactions faster and more securely. This technology allows customers to verify their identities quickly, reducing the time and effort required to complete transactions. An illustration of this is Panera's implementation of Amazon One's palm-based payment system at their outlets. The system asks customers to scan their palms, granting Panera employees the ability to address customers by name, suggest their regular orders, and allow payment by scanning their palms once more.

Moving forward, digital touchpoints will likely continue to replace some humans in this scenario, where their primary function is facilitating transactions. In this touchpoint category, full automation may ultimately become the endgame, contributing to the frictionless experience component.

Scenario 2: Human Engagement Bridges the Trust Gap

Customers making big-ticket purchases, such as buying a new car or house, often research and explore their options to make the best possible choice. In these situations, customers deliberately prolong the discovery stage of the overall decision-making process. Additional "frictions" are necessary to build confidence in their selections.

For example, they may schedule test drives when deciding on a new car or set up home tour appointments when exploring housing options to gain hands-on experience and have conversations with car salespersons or real estate agents. These interactions play a crucial role in building trust, making high-engagement touchpoints a must-have for big-ticket purchases.

While complete digitalization in these scenarios is more challenging, automakers such as Tesla, Volvo, and Ford are moving toward online sales, especially in the case of electric vehicles (EVs). In 2019, Tesla began selling cars entirely online, and Volvo followed suit by selling their EVs exclusively online in 2021. Ford also plans to shift their EV sales to the e-commerce channel.

To help customers decide, these automakers use immersive virtual reality (VR) test drives to allow potential customers to experience the look and feel of the car, complete with 360-degree views, realistic sounds, and even simulated acceleration and braking.

However, it is unlikely that the dealership model will go away entirely due to some state laws that mandate the sale of cars through dealerships. More importantly, customers would not want to eliminate the dealership visit even if they are comfortable with the VR experience. Like the retail industry, physical dealerships will evolve to provide interactions and experiences beyond transactions as a vital supplement to online channels.

The physical touchpoints do not necessarily have to be high cost. For example, Tesla now offers remote test drives to its customers with virtual sales advisors who interact via digital channels. The way it works is that customers can book an appointment on the Tesla website, go to a remote parking space with Tesla vehicles, call Tesla when they arrive, and it will remotely unlock the car for them. The customer can then test drive the vehicle for 30 minutes and drop it off at the exact location.

For this touchpoint category, the digital experience can only partially replace the traditional human experience. While online sales and virtual experiences are becoming more common in big-ticket purchases, in-person touchpoints remain essential for building customer trust and confidence, contributing to the interactive experience component.

Scenario 3: Human Relationship Enhances the Product

In certain situations, particularly with complex products with tangible and intangible aspects, human relationships can enhance the product's value. The delivery of the product, particularly by the individual delivering it, is a critical factor in a customer's decision to buy or use the product.

Furthermore, this aligns with the psychological principle of authority, which states that people tend to follow the guidance of trustworthy, knowledgeable professionals with extensive experience.

Wealth management services are a case in point, where high-net-worth clients receive tailored investment guidance from wealth managers with technical and interpersonal skills. Many factors influence client satisfaction, including the back-end analytics and front-end software that enables wealth management firms to analyze their clients' investments and provide recommendations.

Aside from these tangible products, the human touch in wealth management plays a vital role, providing trustworthy and competent expertise behind financial advice. According to McKinsey, the wealth management industry achieved record-high client retention rates (close to 95 percent) in 2020 due to clients consolidating their financial advisors and strengthening their relationships with their primary, trusted advisors.

In business-to-business (B2B) settings, similar situations frequently arise. Technology companies selling complex products to corporate clients usually employ sales engineers with working knowledge of the products and the skills to present the products. In IBM and Cisco, for instance, sales engineers are responsible for combining their understanding of the client's needs with their knowledge of IBM products. This enables them to provide tailored solutions while maintaining strong client relationships. In other words, the sales engineers are a blend of technical specialists who understand products and sales representatives that build client relationships. When the products have little differentiation, the relationships with sales engineers can be the deciding factor influencing potential customers.

In these industries, companies and customers are co-creating experiences, with most decisions being made together. As a result, the digitization of touchpoints is limited since businesses must facilitate a participative experience where both parties are actively involved. Only a hybrid model that balances digital and in-person touchpoints can achieve this.

One way to do this is through a self-service platform and dashboard that provides customers with 24/7 decision support while supplementing it with remote interactions between company personnel and customers via digital communication channels, which will account for 80 percent of B2B sales interactions between providers and buyers by 2025 (Gartner).

Scenario 4: Human Experience Is the Product

There are scenarios where exceptional customer experience depends heavily on the human touch. It is especially true when the human-to-human connection is the primary motivator for a customer's purchase. Therefore, the success of the companies' offerings hinges on the ability to demonstrate empathy, and the human interface ultimately defines the level of customer satisfaction.

The hospitality industry is an obvious case. This sector has witnessed significant digitalization, with almost 70 percent of travel and tourism bookings in 2022 being made online, according to Statista. Furthermore, the pandemic has accelerated the adoption of contactless technologies for guest-facing activities, such as mobile check-in, digital room keys, and smart room features. However, these advancements were not intended to replace human interaction since hospitality relies on personal connections.

The failure of Henn na, the world's first all-robot-run hotel, demonstrated this digitalization limitation in hospitality. The hotel, which opened in 2015 in Japan, initially had a robot-only staff. However, by 2019, management had to replace half of the robots with human personnel, highlighting that machines cannot adequately serve some touchpoints. Although some Hilton and Marriott hotels also employed robots for contactless room deliveries during the pandemic, human service remained crucial in providing guests with a satisfying experience.

Take the Ritz-Carlton as an example, where every frontline staff member is authorized to exercise their judgment in promptly resolving complicated guest issues or creating delightful experiences for them. As a symbol of empowerment, each staff member can spend up to $2,000 per incident and guest. Even the most advanced AI cannot replicate such discretionary decision making.

Another example is the health care industry. The health care industry, like the hospitality industry, has undergone a significant digital transformation in recent years. Telemedicine, for instance, has gained momentum during the pandemic, providing remote access to care for patients. In addition, electronic medical records offer doctors real-time patient information and provide the data required for artificial intelligence (AI) to assist doctors in making diagnoses and determining treatment options. Moreover, wearables and health tracking via mobile apps provide patients with preventive health care measures.

Despite these digital advancements, health care professionals such as doctors and nurses continue to be vital, especially for long-term treatments. A Kyruus survey in the United States reveals that almost two-thirds of patients consider access to telemedicine as a crucial factor when deciding where to receive health care in the future. However, most patients still prefer in-person care for their long-term health care needs. Interacting with health care professionals gives patients a sense of being cared for and instills confidence that they are in safe hands.

In the hospitality and health care industries, the multisensory experience determines the service quality. While digitalization has brought value in convenience and efficiency in these industries, providing a high-quality human-to-human experience is more important. Interestingly, adopting technologies for administrative tasks in these industries frees up customer-facing staff to interact more with customers, thus augmenting the human experience.

Summary: Fusing Physical and Digital for Complete Immersion

Today, businesses face the challenge of faster commoditization and shorter product life cycle. As a result, they focus on delivering exceptional customer experiences instead of solely competing based on their products. The five elements of a comprehensive immersive customer experience are multisensory, interactive, participative, frictionless, and storytelling experiences. When carefully orchestrated, these components create a fully immersive experience for the customers.

To accomplish this, companies must blend high-tech and high-touch effectively. They need to understand the merits of physical and digital touchpoints and identify scenarios where digital touchpoints can replace physical ones without compromising the immersive customer experience.

REFLECTION QUESTIONS

- How does your company prioritize and balance the human touch and digital experiences in customer interactions? Are there areas that could benefit from increased digitalization or a more personal human connection?

- How can your company orchestrate the whole customer experience to make it more immersive? For example, would you use a multisensory approach or a frictionless experience?

PART II

The Marketing 6.0 Enabler and Environment

CHAPTER 5

Understanding the Tech Enablers

Five Fundamental Technologies Powering Up Metamarketing

Creating engaging experiences that span both physical and digital worlds presents various significant challenges that only technology can address (see Figure 5.1). One of the key challenges is that, as the trends after the pandemic indicate, people are returning to in-person experiences, which means that most customer experiences will likely take place in the physical world in the next few years. Nevertheless, most of the data that businesses collect is digital. Hence, there is a need to find a way to capture these customer experiences in the physical world, convert them into digital data, and provide real-time feedback.

Furthermore, the physical world is three-dimensional, meaning every touchpoint and interaction in the customer experience is also three-dimensional. On the other hand, digital experiences on the Internet are primarily limited to two-dimensional screens. Consequently, there is a need to develop a method for transforming virtual experiences into three-dimensional experiences to integrate physical and digital experiences seamlessly.

Lastly, creating immersive experiences necessitates understanding the audience and collecting comprehensive information about them, ranging from demographic profiles to behaviors. This poses significant privacy and security concerns. Therefore, there is a requirement for a more secure infrastructure to develop and deliver these immersive experiences.

In this chapter, we will explore five essential technologies that assist businesses in overcoming these challenges

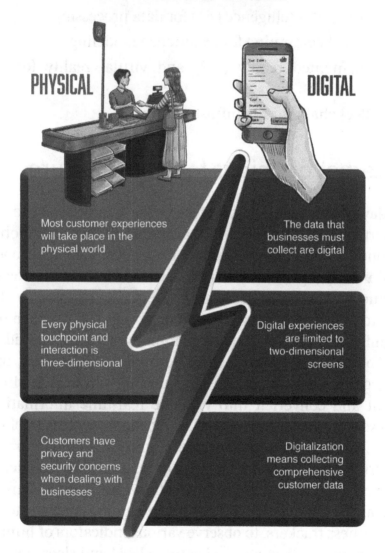

FIGURE 5.1   Three Challenges of Fusing Physical and Digital Experiences.

and enhancing their immersive metamarketing capabilities. These technologies include:

- Internet of Things (IoT) for data capture;
- Artificial intelligence (AI) for data processing;
- Spatial computing for experience modeling;
- Augmented reality (AR) and virtual reality for the interface;
- Blockchain for the infrastructure.

Internet of Things for Data Capture

Today, it is possible to connect virtually any object to the Internet, extending beyond just computers and mobile phones. This includes machines, devices, vehicles, goods, and even people that can interact with one another when connected through a network. The term used to describe this interconnectivity is the Internet of Things (IoT), which has significantly accelerated automation over the past decade.

IoT devices typically come equipped with sensors that can gather data from the surrounding physical environment and convert it into valuable real-time information. These sensors have a range of applications, such as tracking vehicle and goods locations and monitoring temperature in smart homes. Moreover, sensors in retail settings can detect the movements of people and goods within a store. Sensors are also employed in wearables, including smartwatches and fitness trackers, to observe various indicators of human well-being, such as physical activity level and sleep quality, and to detect emergencies such as falls or collisions.

Some IoT devices are also fitted with actuators, which operate in reverse. While sensors capture environmental conditions and convert them into digital data, actuators convert digital data into physical actions. This allows users to control IoT devices and automate specific actions based on the data captured by sensors. For instance, IoT can enable residents of smart homes to remotely or automatically control the temperature depending on weather conditions. With IoT, retailers can also instantly deliver in-app promotion notifications triggered by shoppers strolling down the store aisle.

According to McKinsey's estimation, the global economic potential unlocked by IoT across industries could range from $5.5 trillion to $12.6 trillion by 2030. In addition to automating the operation and maintenance of manufacturing facilities, IoT is expected to generate value by creating immersive customer experiences.

The ability of IoT to monitor and control the physical environments makes it a valuable technology to merge the physical and digital universes. Thus, it is a fundamental technology for creating an immersive experience in retail stores and other physical locations such as customer homes, offices, and vehicles. IoT can incorporate online features into otherwise offline devices, allowing seamless interactions with digital experiences.

As a result, IoT presents an opportunity for marketers to create innovative marketing campaigns that seamlessly integrate online and offline elements. Nivea's *The Protection* campaign is a good illustration of this. The print ad highlights Nivea's commitment to children's sun protection for beach activities and features a paper-thin, detachable bracelet. Children can wear the bracelet, which can be synced with Nivea's mobile app, which notifies parents if their children wander too far while at the beach—further reinforcing the positioning of protection.

Similarly, Heineken launched a campaign in 2022, giving away an IoT device called *The Closer*, which resembles a traditional bottle opener with Heineken branding. The Closer uses a sensor to detect a bottle opening, communicate with the user's device via Bluetooth, and shut down selected work apps. Heineken aimed to address the work-life imbalance with the campaign, encouraging workers to spend some leisure time.

But the most popular use case of IoT for delivering immersive experiences is proximity marketing in retail and food service industries. Major companies such as Walmart, Target, and McDonald's utilize IoT beacons—small, wireless devices that communicate with nearby devices via Bluetooth. These beacons work as a micro-location targeting tool. It allows retailers to detect the presence of specific customers in their outlets and deliver contextual and personalized advertising messages via notifications in their mobile apps.

Most importantly, the beacons serve as a tool for data capture, allowing retailers to get actionable customer insights across online and offline channels. Strategic placement of beacons throughout a retail store, such as near the entrance and every category section, allows for precise customer tracking. Retailers can analyze traffic patterns to optimize the timing of advertising campaigns and monitor customer movement to improve store layout.

The technology also allows retailers to do an accurate cross-channel marketing attribution, which involves identifying the impact of various marketing channels on the customer journey toward a specific goal. With the ability to track both online and offline customer interactions with IoT, marketers can evaluate whether search engine or social media ads resulted in a visit to a physical store and subsequent purchase.

IoT plays a critical role in enabling real-time data capture when providing immersive customer experiences. Although digitalization is increasing, most customer experiences still occur in physical spaces, where most touchpoints remain offline. Traditionally, marketers relied on extensive market research to understand these offline touchpoints. However, IoT offers a new solution that can transform these offline touchpoints into online, allowing marketers to capture a complete picture of the customer journey in real time.

Artificial Intelligence for Data Processing

Artificial intelligence (AI) refers to the ability of computers to replicate human cognitive skills, enabling them to execute tasks that usually require humanlike intelligence, such as problem-solving. Like human intelligence, AI is developed through learning and processing information.

Machine learning—a concept within AI—attempts to emulate this process. By continuously processing disorganized datasets, computers are trained to recognize patterns and create algorithms—rules that connect these datasets. With these algorithms, AI can make predictions and recommend actions. Like humans, AI improves over time by learning from new data and analyzing successful or failed predictions.

Today, AI has become a standard tool for marketers to achieve various objectives. One basic use is to create a low-cost digital interface for customers. By creating AI-powered chatbots, marketers automate responses to basic customer inquiries in sales and customer service processes, in which AI is particularly effective. This frees up human resources to focus on more complex, high-value interactions.

Behind the scenes, marketers use AI to predict consumer behavior. By using AI algorithms built on historical transaction data, marketers can identify customers who are more likely to purchase and have a higher lifetime value. Moreover, AI can predict which product features will be popular in the market and suggest the next product recommended to a particular customer based on their previous purchases. This, in turn, will enhance customer experience.

Over the past few years, PepsiCo has proactively incorporated AI into its marketing efforts to ensure an exceptional buying and consumption experience. For example, PepsiCo leverages AI to produce a customized planogram for each retail channel partner, containing a diagram detailing the optimal placement of specific retail products on shelves or displays to maximize customer purchases. This is achieved with the assistance of a sales representative recording a video of store shelves, which AI will then analyze to develop the planogram.

Another use case of PepsiCo's AI implementation is to ensure a consistent experience of consuming their products. For example, PepsiCo uses AI to formulate the right features of Cheetos to meet customer expectations, from the texture, crunchiness, melting point in the mouth, and curve of the puff, to the quantity of cheese coating.

PepsiCo also drastically reduced the time taken to introduce new products to the market, from years to months, by leveraging AI to analyze millions of social media conversations and quickly detect changes in customer preferences. As a result, products such as Off The Eaten Path's seaweed snacks, Propel's immunity-enhancing bottled water, and Bubbly's flavored sparkling water were developed with features identified by the AI engine.

Generative AI, a type of AI system capable of producing texts, images, and videos in response to prompts—such as Open AI's ChatGPT and DALL-E—is also utilized in advertising and content marketing, where it assists in producing marketing campaigns quickly and on a large scale. This enables personalized marketing at a micro-level, resulting in campaign storytelling that resonates with the audience.

A prime example of this application is Cadbury's #NotJustACadburyAd initiative, which supported local Indian businesses affected by the pandemic. The campaign employed generative AI technology to recreate the face and voice of brand ambassador Shah Rukh Khan, making it seem like he mentioned the names of local businesses in the ads. Small companies could participate by producing their versions of synthetic ads, which amassed over 130,000 ads and garnered 94 million views across various social media platforms.

The most crucial role of AI in immersive marketing, however, is to create a real-time, contextual experience. AI empowers marketers to segment the market into the most granular unit: an individual customer, enabling personalized one-to-one marketing. The significant advantage of AI is its ability to operate in real time, continually capturing data from IoT, learning about customers, and instantly offering the most relevant product or content. This allows marketers to create a highly contextual, immersive experience on the fly.

With the advent of edge AI (a combination of edge computing—defined below—and AI), the processing speed of AI has increased even further. This technology involves processing data closer to its IoT data collection (edge computing) rather than in a remote data center (cloud computing). Doing so allows for faster and higher volume data processing, resulting in real-time actions.

An example is Cooler Screens, a company specializing in in-store digital merchandising and media. Walgreens experimented with Cooler Screens in 2019 by installing coolers that combine IoT and edge AI. These intelligent fridges are equipped with facial detection, eye-tracking, and motion sensors to gather information about the individual standing before the coolers, such as their profile and interests. The screen then displays personalized product recommendations and advertisements.

As of 2023, Cooler Screens has installed over 10,000 screens in retailers such as Kroger, Circle K, and CVS. In addition, it plans to expand its contextual marketing efforts throughout the store by adding smart screens to other surfaces, creating a more immersive in-store experience.

Spatial Computing for Experience Modeling

Spatial computing refers to a group of technologies that manage how humans can intuitively interact with and orchestrate objects in their surroundings. Examples of its practical application are a system that automatically turns on bathroom lights when someone enters at night or activates a factory conveyor belt when a worker places an object on it.

Spatial computing often starts with building digital twins, which are precise digital replicas of physical assets in a virtual environment, often in three-dimensional (3D) models. Digital twins accurately replicate the appearance and function of the original asset and are commonly utilized for real-world modeling and simulation.

Creating digital twins for stores, factories, buildings, and smart cities can help generate insights, plan for improvements, and design the experience within those spaces. Shanghai, and even a small nation like Singapore, already have 3D digital twins, which are used for various purposes such as monitoring traffic flow, planning new developments, and even simulating disaster management.

Spatial computing integrates these 3D digital twins with several key technologies, some of which we have discussed in this chapter. For example, IoT is required to transmit information from the physical world to the digital twin. Shanghai traffic data captured with IoT, for example, is modeled into the digital twin for further analysis on a real-time basis. Digital twin technology uses AI to process these large quantities of sensor data and identify data patterns to generate actionable insights. As a result, governments can visualize, simulate, and create improvements on digital twins and later implement them in the real world.

On a smaller scale, the SoFi Stadium, home to the National Football League (NFL)'s Los Angeles Rams and Los Angeles Chargers, also has a digital twin of the stadium and the surrounding Hollywood Park. The digital twin has proven beneficial in enhancing the guest experience, particularly during major events such as the Super Bowl. For instance, it can detect areas with higher temperatures and promptly address the issue. Moreover, the digital twin is a valuable tool for game-day management, as it allows for streamlined coordination of the thousands of frontline staff operating in various locations throughout the stadium.

Spatial computing is a key technology for simulating experiences, enabling businesses to enhance their planning capabilities. Rather than designing customer experiences in theory, spatial computing allows companies to create visual 3D simulations of their designs, particularly when developing immersive customer experiences.

Spatial computing is also crucial for delivering an immersive customer experience that seamlessly integrates physical and digital interfaces. For example, in the fashion and beauty industry, it is used in retail stores to provide customers with a more interactive and immersive shopping experience. An illustration of this is the use of spatial computing in smart fitting rooms piloted by fashion brands such as Ralph Lauren, American Eagle Outfitters, and COS.

Smart fitting rooms utilize spatial computing to instantly recognize the clothing items that customers bring into the room and provide personalized recommendations for products and styling. With the 3D visuals, shoppers can do virtual try-ons from multiple angles, even for items that are not currently available in stores but can be ordered for delivery.

The virtual try-ons are also popular with beauty retailers. For example, Sephora has the Virtual Artist app, which scans the face and lets customers try on makeup virtually, available on mobile phones and in select stores. Similarly, L'Oréal uses a virtual try-on called Style My Hair, which allows consumers to try out different haircuts, colors, and styles virtually.

The application of spatial computing to deliver such experiences is related to interface technologies such as virtual reality (VR) and augmented reality (AR).

Augmented Reality and Virtual Reality for the Interface

The development of immersive experiences that combine physical and digital worlds heavily relies on the human-machine interface (HMI) field, which explores ways for humans to interact with machines. Although people navigate three-dimensional physical worlds, most interactions with technology and digital content occur on two-dimensional screens. Consequently, the latest interface trend involves three-dimensional technologies such as virtual reality (VR) and augmented reality (AR), which aim to bridge this gap.

Both AR and VR use spatial computing technology. VR technology replaces the user's view of the physical world with a simulated virtual environment by utilizing head-mounted displays that block their field of view. This results in a completely immersive experience that does not allow users to interact with their physical surroundings.

On the other hand, AR overlays digital content onto the user's real-world view without completely obstructing their field of view. To experience AR, users commonly use either mobile phones or specialized glasses. This technology enables users to interact with digital elements while still being aware of and engaging with their physical surroundings. What the user sees is partly digital and partly real. In essence, while VR provides a wholly digital immersive experience, AR combines physical and digital experiences.

Both AR and VR create a more immersive experience. Particularly when combined with digital twin technology, the digital components in AR and VR become more realistic. For example, in AR, digital twins can be used to project virtual objects onto the real-world environment in a way that accurately matches their physical properties. In VR, digital twins can create accurate and realistic simulations of real-world settings, such as buildings, cars, and cities.

While AR and VR technologies are changing how we interact with digital content, their trajectories differ. VR technology is primarily used for corporate purposes, partly due to the high cost and inconvenience of the devices for daily consumer use. Specifically, VR is used for hands-on training that requires role-play and skill-building experiences, such as training for surgeons, pilots, welders, and customer service associates.

As an illustration, Walmart has utilized VR courses to train more than a million frontline staff. For example, one course teaches them how to operate The Pickup Tower, a large kiosk that enables customers to retrieve their online orders. Previously, the training for this process involved an entire day of in-store training. However, with the implementation of VR technology, training time has been reduced to just 15 minutes without any reduction in effectiveness.

Conversely, AR has a bigger potential for consumer use and is better for marketing activations. The popularity of AR can be attributed, in part, to the success of games such as Pokémon Go. This game allows players to interact with virtual creatures that appear present in their actual environment when viewed through a mobile app. However, the true advantage of AR over VR lies in its utilization of mobile phones, which are ubiquitous, and its ability to enable users to interact with both physical and digital environments.

AR is revolutionizing product demos and tryouts during the discovery phase of the customer journey. By allowing customers to virtually experience how products will look and function in a real-life setting before making a purchase, they gain greater confidence in their decision. This technology is applicable across various industries, from beauty to footwear and furniture. Brands such as Clinique, Vans, and

IKEA use AR to showcase their products in three dimensions, with complete customization options for their target audience.

The advantages of AR and VR are often combined in mixed reality (MR). While AR superimposes digital content onto the physical world, MR takes it a step further by allowing the digital element to interact with the physical space, resulting in a more immersive experience. MR falls between AR and the fully immersive VR, offering more complex physical-digital interactions than AR while maintaining the real-world context that is missing in VR (see Figure 5.2).

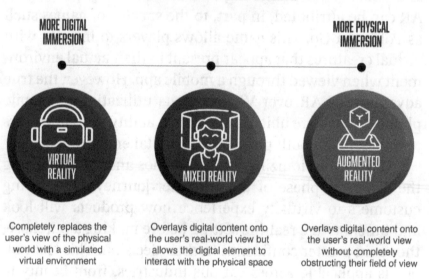

FIGURE 5.2 The Spectrum of Physical-Digital Interfaces.

An example of an MR application for marketing is Chipotle's Giant Burrito ad, aired live during a National Hockey League (NHL) playoff game. The ad seamlessly integrated a commercial break with live programming by projecting digital content on the jumbotron, creating the illusion of a Chipotle-branded Zamboni bringing a giant burrito bowl on the ice during the live camera feed. The ad then demonstrated the interaction between the overlaid digital content and the real-world ice rink by showing a giant gloved hand breaking through the ice and grabbing the bowl displayed on the jumbotron.

Procter & Gamble's Gillette did similar MR activation before a National Football League (NFL) game at the Gillette Stadium. During the live broadcast, the audience could see on the screen an enormous virtual razor built at midfield.

The immersive technology interface makes connecting digital content and messages with real-world context easier. As customers return to live events and physical spaces post-pandemic, these hybrid and immersive experiences have become a trend among advertisers.

Blockchain for the Infrastructure

In recent years, blockchain has been considered a major technological innovation, reshaping how businesses operate. Many technology professionals view blockchain as the next game-changer, following AI. In fact, blockchain technology appears to be a natural solution to privacy issues arising from the growing use of AI since it provides a secure infrastructure for customers to interact with the Internet.

At its core, blockchain is a decentralized database that records encrypted data across multiple computers rather than in a central location. Each computer in the network has a copy of the entire database, and any changes made to the database must be validated across all computers, making it highly secure from cyberattacks and fraud. In addition, since all data are visible from every computer in the network, it also increases the transparency of transactions.

By providing a secure and transparent system, blockchain eliminates the requirement for intermediaries to moderate and reconcile transactions, facilitating a direct relationship between the parties involved. This leads to overall efficiency and facilitates the exchange of a wide range of assets, including virtual items and intangible properties.

Blockchain is predominantly used as an infrastructure technology, with most business applications at the backend. For example, Walmart has implemented blockchain to manage invoices and payments to third-party logistics partners, resulting in a significant decrease in invoice disputes from 70 percent to less than 1 percent.

In the marketing space, blockchain technology is utilized to track the series of transactions from advertisers to media publishers and identify areas of inefficiencies. Toyota, for instance, implemented blockchain to optimize its media buying for its advertising campaign placements, leading to a 30 to 35 percent reduction in total advertising spend.

The implementation of blockchain technology on the front end remains somewhat contentious. The ability of blockchain to facilitate transactions without intermediaries has given rise to groundbreaking concepts such as cryptocurrencies and non-fungible tokens (NFTs). A cryptocurrency is a digital currency that operates without central authority, such as a government or bank. Although it offers the benefits of efficient transactions, most cryptocurrencies lack intrinsic value, making them highly speculative and volatile.

Another controversial use case is the NFT, which serves as a unique digital certificate of asset ownership. Typically, NFTs record ownership of digital files like artworks, photos, videos, and audio on the blockchain. These assets can be traded and allow the original owner to receive royalties for future reselling of the assets. However, similar to cryptocurrencies, NFTs representing digital collectibles and artworks are speculative assets often traded at irrational prices.

Blockchain—especially cryptocurrencies and NFTs—is at the heart of the immersive metaverse experience. A metaverse is a simulated and immersive virtual world that allows users to engage in various activities, much like in the physical world. It may appear to be simply a virtual game platform for entertainment. However, when a metaverse is supported by blockchain technology, it operates as a fully functional economy with its currency and commerce system for exchanging virtual goods. Users can utilize cryptocurrencies to trade digital assets, such as metaverse lands, cars, and clothes, while all ownership is certified through NFTs.

Leading brands are already investing in building a presence in metaverses. For example, Coca-Cola was among the first brands to launch NFT-based collectibles in the metaverse in 2021. The company released a collection of NFT-based collectibles featuring various virtual items such as a vintage cooler, a jacket, an audio disc, and a set of trading cards that included dynamic motion, movement, and multisensorial elements. Coca-Cola also aims to integrate the digital offering with physical collectibles, as the highest bidder would also receive the physical cooler stocked with bottles of Coca-Cola.

Nike has also entered the metaverse through Nikeland, a virtual world within a video game platform that offers an immersive 3D space featuring its headquarters as the backdrop. In Nikeland, users can personalize their avatars and engage in games where their offline movements translate into in-game moves.

Nike has also launched ".Swoosh," a blockchain-powered virtual community and marketplace for virtual creators where members can collaborate to create virtual products such as shoes or jerseys, access physical products, or have private conversations with athletes or designers. But perhaps Nike's collaboration with its recently acquired RTFKT represents the most significant step toward integrating the physical and digital worlds. The two companies are creating virtual designs that will be brought to life by releasing their physical counterpart shoes.

It is worth mentioning that the advancement of blockchain technology for immersive metaverses is ongoing, and numerous brands are still experimenting with it. Therefore, there is still a long way to go.

This is similar to the development of AI, which has been controversial for many years. Advocates of AI emphasized its numerous benefits, while skeptics pointed out privacy issues and its imperfections. Only with the recent emergence of ChatGPT has AI reached a tipping point and become widely used.

While the short-term potential of blockchain-powered metaverses is uncertain, there is no doubt that they have a promising future. Brands experimenting with metaverses are discovering that younger customers are highly interested in them. Metaverses are three-dimensional and immersive versions of social media platforms for these customers. Consequently, brands seeking to engage younger generations are still cautiously adopting metaverses.

Summary: Five Fundamental Technologies Powering Up Metamarketing

There are various challenges to creating immersive experiences that combine physical and digital worlds, such as converting physical experiences into digital data, transforming virtual experiences into three-dimensional experiences, and ensuring privacy and security. However, these issues can be addressed through the utilization of five technologies.

The Internet of Things (IoT) and artificial intelligence (AI) enable the capture and processing of physical interactions in real time. Moreover, spatial computing and immersive interfaces, such as virtual reality (VR) and augmented reality (AR), enable businesses to seamlessly blend three-dimensional digital experiences with physical ones. Finally, blockchain technology offers a secure and transparent infrastructure for providing immersive customer experiences to address privacy and security concerns (see Figure 5.3).

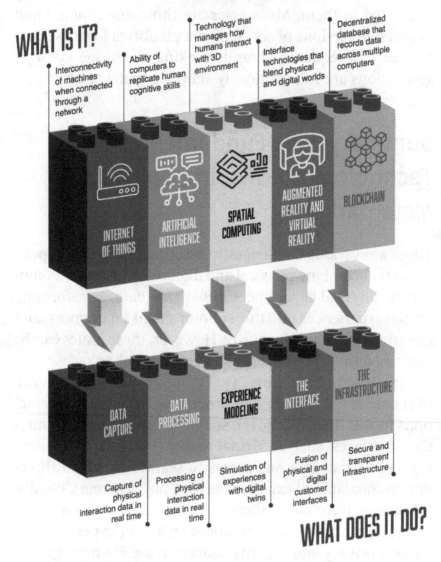

FIGURE 5.3 Five Fundamental Technologies Powering Up Metamarketing.

REFLECTION QUESTIONS

- How is your company currently utilizing the five technologies to create immersive experiences that combine physical and digital worlds? Are there any areas where you could be doing more?

- Will utilizing blockchain technology to construct a metaverse reach a tipping point in the next few years? Do you believe that virtual-only customer experiences in the metaverse have a future going forward?

CHAPTER 6

Building Extended Realities

The Immersive Experience in Real Life

D espite the significant growth of e-commerce, physical retail channels continue to dominate sales. In fact, e-commerce only accounted for less than 15 percent of total retail sales in the United States in 2022 (US Department of Commerce). Similarly, in China, the world's largest e-commerce market, e-commerce's share of total retail sales is still below 30 percent (Euromonitor).

Even technology giants such as Apple and Amazon, recognizing this trend, continue to prioritize their brick-and-mortar strategies alongside e-commerce. Apple, renowned for its customer experience–centric approach to its products, extends this philosophy to its physical stores. In fact, Apple holds the distinction of having the highest annual sales per square foot among retailers, generating an impressive $5,500 compared to Tiffany & Co.'s second-place figure of $2,900 (based on CoStar report).

Meanwhile, Amazon consistently explores and strengthens its presence in the physical retail space. The record-breaking acquisition of Whole Foods in 2017 exemplifies this commitment, with Amazon subsequently expanding the chain to more locations and enhancing the shopping experience by implementing Amazon checkout technology. Furthermore, Amazon has experimented with various store formats under its brand, such as the food-focused Amazon Go, grocery-centric Amazon Fresh, and fashion-oriented Amazon Style. By closing underperforming stores and opening new ones in good locations, Amazon actively seeks to refine its physical retail strategy.

Apple and Amazon have also extensively utilized out-of-home (OOH) media in their marketing campaigns to attract customers and bolster their retail store strategies. In fact, according to the OOH Advertising Association of America, these two companies rank among the top five advertisers in the OOH, which includes billboards, transit media, and outdoor spots.

Current trends suggest that physical channels will remain favorable in the coming years. Recent studies indicate that customers are returning to shopping in physical stores as pandemic restrictions ease and as they may have suffered digital fatigue in the last few years. For instance, a survey by Mood Media found that 71 percent of customers worldwide are now shopping in physical stores as frequently as, if not more than, before the pandemic.

The trend toward physical shopping seems to apply even to younger demographics. For example, McKinsey revealed that despite buying many things online, Generation Z is more likely to do brick-and-mortar shopping than Generation Y across 25 categories. Additionally, A.S. Watson's research shows that Generation Z prefers to buy products in-store for categories where social interaction is essential, such as the beauty industry.

These statistics indicate the continued significance of physical retail spaces, which remain central to most customer experiences. As a result, it may be more crucial to focus on creating immersive environments in the real world rather than solely in virtual realms such as the metaverse. This approach is commonly referred to by younger generations as IRL marketing in contrast to URL marketing. IRL stands for "in real life," highlighting interactions in physical spaces. On the other hand, URL (uniform resource locator, a technical term for a web address) refers to online interactions through digital channels.

IRL marketing covers a range of settings where customers are present and spend time, such as retail stores, pop-up shops, restaurants, OOH advertising, brand activations, corporate events, showrooms, and experience centers. These locations offer valuable chances for direct interactions and engagements with customers.

Reinventing the Third Place

The concept of an ideal IRL space traces back to the late 1980s when sociologist Ray Oldenburg coined the term "the third place." It refers to a physical location away from the home (the first place) and the workplace (the second place) that provides social experiences. While the home offers a private sanctuary and the office provides a formal environment, the third place offers a more communal atmosphere. Examples include cafes, restaurants, bookstores, bars, gyms, malls, public libraries, and parks.

The third place is usually an inclusive space accessible to regular and new visitors from diverse socioeconomic backgrounds, as the entry cost is either zero or affordable for most people. Its primary focus is social interaction, providing an environment where people can converse and build connections. Therefore, the ambiance is welcoming and often playful (see Figure 6.1).

Various brands have successfully embraced the third-place concept in the last few decades. Starbucks, for instance,

WHAT IS THE THIRD PLACE?

FIGURE 6.1   The Definition of the Third Place.

has long been synonymous with the idea, as its stores have evolved into social hubs where people hang out and socialize with friends. The chain offers comfortable chairs, ambient music, and decorations that make people stay. The chain was also one of the first to provide free Wi-Fi and charging outlets, allowing visitors to spend more time at the stores.

Fast-food restaurants such as McDonald's have also become popular third-place options for specific demographics in the United States, particularly senior citizens and low-income communities. Affordable food and complimentary Wi-Fi attract these groups to McDonald's, where they can forge connections with one another.

Apple Stores adopt a "modern town square" philosophy that aligns with the third-place concept. Through strategic locations and beautiful designs, Apple repurposes its stores as semipublic spaces, inviting customers to gather with their communities. Central to this concept is the "Today at Apple" program, which hosts creative skills classes, such as photography or coding sessions, aiming to bring people together and discover new skills. These free lessons can be seen as a way for Apple to reduce barriers to using its premium products and allow more people to experience them.

Today, the younger generations have assigned the digital space the role of a third place. They devote a lot of time to social media and virtual worlds to connect with familiar and new friends. While they may physically be present at local establishments such as Starbucks and McDonald's, their attention is fully immersed in the virtual realm.

In fact, they have a very different perspective on the third place as they are accustomed to working from anywhere with the help of digital office technologies. Unlike previous generations, they may not perceive a clear distinction between their home and work environments, rendering the traditional notion of the third place less relevant.

However, this behavior raises concerns about their well-being. According to Cigna US Loneliness Index, Generation Z is the loneliest generation, with 73 percent reporting loneliness. Furthermore, a survey conducted by Harmony Healthcare IT has revealed alarming statistics: 42 percent of Generation Z individuals have been diagnosed with mental health issues, and a staggering 85 percent experience anxiety about their future.

The survey further highlights the impact of the pandemic on those anxiety levels, as the restrictions and lockdowns have significantly curtailed in-person interactions and socialization opportunities. It turns out that even for the younger generations, engaging with others in physical spaces remains crucial for their happiness.

Indeed, humans are inherently social beings. Despite technological advancements, social connection remains an essential and timeless human need. It serves as a reminder that the primary purpose of a physical location is to facilitate and nurture social relationships. If a place fails to fulfill this role, its value diminishes. Consequently, retail establishments that prioritize mere transactions run the risk of being overshadowed by the convenience and efficiency of e-commerce.

Nevertheless, it's important to note that third spaces can still incorporate digital elements. In fact, PwC's Global Consumer Insights Pulse Survey revealed that customers expect the physical shopping experience to be enhanced, facilitated, or mediated by digital technologies.

When physical settings are combined with digital elements, we refer to it as an "extended reality" (XR). XR is a technical term encompassing augmented reality (AR), virtual reality (VR), and mixed reality (MR) as the three physical-digital interfaces. However, the term can also refer to IRL environments that are augmented with digital experiences, extending the boundaries of the physical realm.

There are five approaches to incorporating digital technologies into physical spaces and creating these extended realities, resulting in a more immersive customer experience (see Figure 6.2).

Seamless Transactions

One of the main challenges associated with physical spaces is the considerable time required to complete transactions, as evidenced by long queues and time-consuming checkouts. However, businesses can address this issue by incorporating innovative technologies that streamline the transaction process.

For instance, Amazon Go introduced a smart checkout system now available to other retailers through Amazon Web Services. Once installed in a store, this system identifies shoppers' identities and automatically captures their digital payment information. Furthermore, it utilizes advanced technology to recognize the items shoppers pick from the shelves. As a result, customers are instantly charged for the things they take and can conveniently check out from the store, receiving digital receipts for their purchases.

Another noteworthy example is the concept of contactless commerce, exemplified by Nike's Speed Shop in their

EXTENDING
THE PHYSICAL REALITIES

SEAMLESS TRANSACTIONS
Examples: smart checkout, contactless payment

CONTEXTUAL RECOMMENDATIONS
Examples: virtual fitting room, mood reader

INTERACTIVE ENGAGEMENTS
Examples: interactive display, in-store gamification

AUGMENTED DISCOVERIES
Examples: QR and in-store app mode, digital wayfinding

PRE- AND POST-EXPERIENCES
Examples: mobile app integration

FIGURE 6.2   Bringing Digital Technologies to the Third Place.

flagship store in New York. With this approach, customers reserve shoes online and are assigned a designated locker at the store. Then, using their mobile phones, they can unlock their assigned locker, try on the desired shoes, and purchase without waiting in line. This approach follows a buy online, pick-up in store (BOPIS) model, offering customers a convenient and time-saving shopping experience.

The rise of e-commerce has brought about a heightened customer expectation that transactions should be convenient and hassle-free. As a result, transactions are often seen as the least important touchpoint in the customer journey within physical channels, and customers desire to minimize the time spent on them.

However, ironically, transactions often become the most painful touchpoint, taking away valuable time from more meaningful interactions that physical spaces offer. Therefore, implementing frictionless technology becomes a hygiene factor in enhancing the overall customer experience in physical environments.

Contextual Recommendations

The rise of social media and e-commerce has fostered a demand for personalized experiences. The younger generations—considered artificial intelligence natives—have grown accustomed to receiving tailored content and product suggestions that perfectly align with their preferences.

Currently, in-store experiences lag when it comes to personalization. However, businesses have the opportunity to embrace digital technologies to bring about in-store personalization. This entails providing tailored messages and offers to customers throughout their in-store journey.

An illustration of this is the virtual fitting room, which has been adopted by fashion brands such as Ralph Lauren and COS. By harnessing technologies such as augmented reality (AR) and the Internet of Things (IoT), these fitting rooms can identify the items customers bring in and provide personalized styling suggestions. The customers can virtually try on the suggested items and explore various color options, complementary clothing pieces, and accessories. Moreover, customers can quickly request assistance by pressing a button whenever needed.

Another groundbreaking implementation is UMOOD by Uniqlo in Australia. The device uses neural technology to read customers' emotions and recommend T-shirts based on their moods. Customers wear a neuro-headset that analyzes their brainwaves while they watch different stimuli. A custom-built algorithm then analyzes their neurological responses to determine their current mood and suggest the ideal T-shirt.

Implementing personalized in-store experiences can act as a strong differentiation in increasingly commoditized industries, such as apparel. In these industries, products often face imitations and price cuts. Companies can effectively avoid this commoditization by leveraging personalization, especially when supported by customer data.

Furthermore, personalization is essential in product categories that present customers with an overwhelming array of options, making it challenging to find the right product in-store without technological assistance. In a world with content overload, the ability to engage directly with customers and offer tailored recommendations becomes increasingly valuable.

Interactive Engagements

With the widespread use of smartphones, people have become accustomed to navigating digital interfaces through touch and swipe gestures. Furthermore, as digital products and services have gained popularity through mobile apps, interacting with screens has become second nature to most people.

Physical spaces can also embrace interactivity by offering user interfaces and experiences that leverage people's familiarity with digital screen media. Bloomingdale, for instance, tested out interactive window displays for Ralph Lauren's promotion featuring large touch screens. Passersby could interact with the screens and change the product images displayed. In addition, they could use an interactive mobile app to buy selected items.

Similarly, Timberland also explored a similar approach but with a slight variation, using hand gestures to navigate through the digital interface. This enables passersby to use the touchless try-on feature for every product inside the store without entering, ultimately attracting more foot traffic.

Retailers can also leverage their familiarity with mobile apps to create interactive experiences. Mobile apps are practical tools for implementing gamification strategies. A good example is Burberry's Shenzhen store, which collaborated with the popular Chinese messaging app WeChat to introduce in-store gamification. Customers who are members of the store's loyalty program can collect "social currency" as they explore and interact with in-store exhibitions. These accumulated points can then be redeemed for exclusive rewards, including upgraded avatars, access to a secret dining menu, VIP events, and entry to a hidden room.

As customers now spend significant time with screens and crave interactivity, their shopping habits have shifted from browsing physical shelves to scrolling through digital pages. To compete with e-commerce websites, physical spaces must adopt similar user interfaces and experiences that customers are accustomed to.

Augmented Discoveries

Being pragmatic, younger generations carefully assess products and compare them against alternatives before making buying decisions. The emergence of e-commerce has simplified this process by offering convenient access to comprehensive product details, customer reviews, and price comparisons. Accessing such information is easier than seeking assistance from in-store staff, granting e-commerce an advantage over physical stores.

Moreover, information such as customer reviews is considered more trustworthy than sales pitches made by store attendants. As a result, customers often adopt the "showrooming" approach, using their smartphones to research products while in-store. Due to its convenience, customers may purchase the product online (instead of in-store) shortly after conducting their research, creating a missed opportunity for the store.

It is now possible to incorporate information discovery into the in-store experience to address these issues. One approach involves the utilization of mobile apps with in-store modes. These apps enable customers to scan QR codes next to each product. By doing so, customers gain access to comprehensive information about the products, akin to the experience of online shopping. Furthermore, customers can check out the products with store-only promotions on the retailer's mobile app, preventing them from buying the product on e-commerce platforms. Retailers using this approach include Best Buy and Home Depot.

By leveraging the detailed product information available through the app, these retailers can also strategically suggest complementary items or accessories that go hand-in-hand with the scanned product. For example, a customer scanning a television might be presented with recommendations for sound systems, wall mounts, or streaming devices. This cross-merchandising strategy increases the chances of additional sales and helps customers discover and conveniently purchase all the necessary components in one shopping trip.

Another approach to the in-store discovery tool is digital wayfinding, as implemented by big-box retailers such as Home Depot and Lowe's. These retailers utilize AR-enabled store wayfinding systems that provide store maps and guide customers to specific sections where they can find the product they are looking for.

Additionally, some apps incorporate visual product search functionality. With this feature, consumers can simply take a picture of a product they are interested in, and the app instantly searches the product catalog and directs customers to the exact or similar product. These approaches help make the in-store experience more suitable for younger generations and enable companies to bridge the gap between the physical and digital realms.

Pre- and Post-Experience

The final aspect to consider when enhancing the physical space through technology is ensuring its seamless integration with people's digital lifestyle, even when they are outside the physical environment. Businesses should proactively anticipate visitors' experiences before they enter the premises and extend the engagement long after they have left. By doing so, companies can sustain customer engagement over time.

One practical approach is integrating the physical-digital experience with mobile apps, as they serve as a ubiquitous tool that accompanies customers inside and outside the physical space. Various digital features found in-store can be incorporated into a mobile app, enabling customers to replicate the experience wherever they go.

Nike, for instance, has experimented with Nike Live, a members-only concept store that places the mobile app at the core of the store experience. The store encourages users to utilize the mobile app for special collection access and in-store community engagements. Furthermore, the app collects valuable customer data, empowering Nike to tailor their product offerings and store activities. For example, Nike adjusts its merchandise biweekly to align with the evolving preferences of the surrounding neighborhood. This emphasis on local communities and member engagement embodies the essence of the third-place concept.

As Generation Z and Generation Alpha embrace the physical-digital (phygital) lifestyle, connecting experiences in both realms becomes imperative. This approach caters to the shopping preferences of these young generations while encouraging them to maintain in-person interactions, which are beneficial for their overall well-being.

Designing Immersive Third Places

When creating an IRL space, it is crucial to consider the central theme because each design element conveys a message. Take, for instance, the vibrant yellow and red hues of McDonald's eateries, which symbolize happiness and a growing appetite. Conversely, the Apple Store's floor-to-ceiling transparent glass panels epitomize a sleek and minimalist aesthetic. When these elements are combined, they create an overall impression that influences perceptions toward the space's owner.

Hence, through specific spatial design, brands can communicate their positioning and brand values. For businesses striving to create exceptional third spaces, it is crucial to skillfully manage and orchestrate these elements to ensure a consistent and cohesive brand narrative. In essence, space design is an excellent avenue for storytelling and acts somewhat like subtle advertising.

Each element in a physical space is also a stimulus that triggers a response. When visitors enter an area, their minds process these multiple stimuli almost simultaneously. As a result, it will evoke certain emotions, such as joy, excitement, or relaxation. These emotions prepare the visitors for subsequent interactive touchpoints. For instance, a less intimidating ambiance combined with medical credibility cues in a hospital setting may alleviate patient fear.

Most importantly, these stimuli influence customer behavior throughout their journey, from enticing people to enter a store to exploring products and ultimately making purchases. In addition, different spatial arrangements elicit varying impacts on behavior. Comfortable seating paired with relaxing coffeehouse music, for example, invites people to stay longer, while limited seating and standing desks accompanied by upbeat music discourage lingering.

Every element within the physical environment serves multiple objectives, including functional and artistic aspects. A seating area, for example, has a clear function, but the type of seats chosen can significantly impact the overall tone of the space and elicit different responses. A leather sofa, for instance, creates a perception of luxury, while stools contribute to a casual ambiance. Likewise, a long table with six chairs fosters a sense of community and togetherness, whereas a single table and chair are more inviting to individuals seeking solitude.

In essence, a physical space consists of three essential components that collaboratively narrate a story, evoke emotions, and influence behavior. They are physical evidence, processes, and people. When effectively orchestrated, these elements converge to create an immersive IRL experience that leaves a lasting impression and makes a significant business impact (see Figure 6.3).

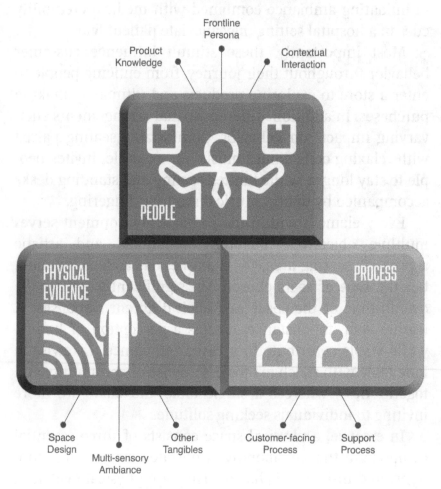

FIGURE 6.3   Components of the In-Real-Life Experience.

Physical Evidence

Physical evidence encompasses tangible cues that define the space, with the most prominent aspect being the space design itself. For example, an IKEA store is characterized by showrooms replicating various home sections, such as living rooms, workspaces, kitchens, bedrooms, and dining areas. The layout is carefully arranged to guide customers along a predetermined path, ensuring they go through all these sections.

The journey typically concludes in the market hall, where IKEA offers accessories, and the self-serve area, where customers can obtain the products they have encountered in the showrooms. Additionally, the store provides a communal space in the form of a restaurant and café.

Physical evidence also encompasses multisensory elements that complement the visual design. Background music and ambient scents are among the most common examples. For instance, Starbucks is renowned for curating its playlists across various genres, from coffeehouse tunes to upbeat summer hip-hop. The brand also promotes a signature coffee aroma, which is vital in defining its store experience.

Additionally, physical evidence includes other supporting tangibles such as employee uniforms, branded merchandise, and business cards. These tangible elements convey clear signals to customers about the purpose of the space and, more importantly, the brand's essence. Therefore, it is crucial for brands to carefully select physical evidence that effectively represents what they stand for.

Process

In a physical customer experience setting, there are two types of processes. The first type is customer-facing processes, which are visible and directly experienced by customers. These processes typically mirror the customer journey, encompassing the various touchpoints within the space.

For instance, in a typical Starbucks store experience, customers queue in line, place orders, make payments, and receive drinks. Some customers may even enjoy observing their drink being prepared by the barista due to the open brewing area.

On the other hand, some processes occur behind the scenes, hidden from the customers' view but essential for delivering the desired customer experience. For example, staff members prepare coffee inventories, ensure the equipment is in order, and set up the point-of-sale (POS) system each morning before the store opens its doors to customers.

Both types of processes are vital components of the customer experience. Failure in a single step can have a ripple effect on subsequent stages of the customer journey. To design effective processes, companies must study how customers navigate the space and interact with its elements.

While physical evidence can be regarded as the props that define the space, the process drives the overall operation of the space. It provides clarity and coordination regarding how customers interact with other elements within the space, including physical evidence and the final component: people.

People

The most crucial component is people, distinguishing an IRL experience from a URL experience. This element is why a virtual space can never fully replicate an ideal third place and why e-commerce faces challenges in replacing in-person retailing.

The role of people varies depending on the level of engagement. In high-engagement scenarios, interactions with people become the most significant aspect of the customer experience (refer to Chapter 4 for the human experience spectrum). However, even in low-engagement scenarios where customers do not anticipate direct interactions with company staff, the people component remains essential, particularly when it comes to problem-solving during instances such as handling complaints.

The people component poses the greatest challenge and has consequently emerged as a significant differentiator that is difficult to replicate. To align with the physical evidence and processes, companies must recruit individuals with personas that harmonize with the other two elements. For instance, minimalist space with streamlined processes necessitates individuals who are agile and skilled problem solvers.

In some cases, finding an exact match for the desired persona may be a daunting task, requiring companies to invest in training their personnel over time to achieve the desired objective. The necessary skills often encompass technical expertise, such as product knowledge, and interpersonal abilities, such as delivering personalized service.

Airline cabin crew exemplify this, with one flight attendant typically serving around 50 passengers in the minimalist space of an aircraft. They are personal problem solvers, addressing situations such as unanticipated dietary requirements by finding suitable alternatives onboard. Their expertise is also often tested in handling unexpected scenarios such as medical emergencies or turbulence. The cabin crew's skills and expertise can differentiate the overall airline experience. For instance, Singapore Airlines and its renowned "Singapore Girl" cabin crew enhance the customer experience with Asian hospitality, consistently winning top cabin crew awards.

With effective management, people can synergize with physical evidence and processes to deliver a cohesive storytelling experience to customers. The Singapore Girl serves as a prime example, where the flight attendants play a pivotal role in defining the brand, perhaps even more so than the modern aircrafts and the efficient booking process.

Summary: The Immersive Experience in Real Life

Despite the growing e-commerce, physical retail channels remain central to the overall customer experience. Therefore, it becomes increasingly vital to prioritize the creation of immersive environments in the real world rather than focusing solely on virtual realms such as the metaverse. The concept of an ideal physical space is closely tied to the notion of the "third place," which refers to a physical location separate from home and work that offers social experiences.

To enhance the customer experience further, it is essential to integrate digital technologies into physical spaces and establish these extended realities. Companies should incorporate digital features within physical stores, such as seamless transactions, contextual recommendations, interactive engagement, augmented discoveries, and extended experiences. By doing so, businesses can create a more immersive customer experience in real life.

REFLECTION QUESTIONS

- Do you sell your products and services through physical locations? Review the physical evidence, process, and people, and evaluate whether you have created a coherent brand story.
- What are some ideas you have to integrate digital technologies into the physical locations and make them more immersive?

CHAPTER 7

Tapping into the Metaverse

The Future Form of Social Media Platforms

The current social media format emerged in the early 2000s and gained momentum as the Internet, personal computers, and smartphones became widely prevalent. Since then, social media has become a cornerstone of the second Internet iteration, or Web2.

Web2 represents a crucial evolution of the Internet, enabling the platform economy. Unlike in the Web1 era, where users could only consume content, Web2 allows users to produce and share content through social media. This marked the rise of user-generated content on the Internet.

Throughout the Web2 upsurge, we have witnessed the ascent and decline of various social media, including Friendster, Myspace, and Google+. During this period, we have seen the evolution of how social media work as platforms. The prominent social media today, such as Facebook and Instagram (both are part of Meta), TikTok, and Twitter, enable users to connect and generate and distribute multimedia content. They typically generate revenue by providing a platform for advertisers to market products and services.

Over the past 20 years, social media has undergone major shifts, leading to present-day challenges. Initially intended for friends and acquaintances to connect, social media has evolved into an alternative form of mass media that reaches a similarly large audience. The growth of the user base has partly contributed to this shift, along with social platforms attempting to fulfill big advertisers' demands for large audience targeting to improve reach.

Unlike traditional mass media, large social media platforms have access to massive amounts of personal data, which goes beyond location and demographic data to include users' interests and behaviors, enabling the platforms to create detailed user profiles. This data is valuable to advertisers for precise micro-targeting and personalization, but it also raises data protection and privacy concerns.

Many social media users protect their privacy using pseudonyms and not sharing real photos on their profiles. The anonymity allowed on social networks largely depends on the platform. Some platforms, such as Facebook, require users to identify themselves by their real names. Despite this, Facebook has still had to shut down billions of fake accounts over the years.

While anonymity may protect some users from privacy issues, it can also lead to negative consequences. Unlike traditional media, social media content is mainly unmoderated, as content creators are free to post whatever they want to generate engagement. However, this lack of accountability may lead to abusive tactics such as spreading fake news, misinformation, cyberbullying, and hate speech.

The metaverse, considered the symbol of Web3, or the next iteration of the Internet, seems to be the logical next step for the evolution of social media, and it can potentially address some of its issues. According to a survey conducted by Accenture, most users want the metaverse to provide a safer environment than social media. However, at the current state, 55 percent of respondents believed the level of safety would be indifferent, and only 22 percent thought metaverse was better than social media.

Undeniably, the metaverse is still developing toward its ideal state. According to a study conducted by Pew Research Center and Elon University's Imagining the Internet Center, 54 percent of technology experts anticipate the metaverse will become much more refined by 2040, influencing the lifestyle of over half a billion people worldwide.

Besides offering a more immersive experience than social media, metaverses have the potential to provide better security and privacy, primarily via blockchain technology. With blockchain, users can have greater control over their data and enjoy enhanced security. However, how the metaverse will effectively tackle the challenge of moderating harmful content remains uncertain.

What Is the Metaverse?

The concept of the metaverse is still relatively new in the business world. It gained significant attention in 2021–2022, partly due to Facebook's rebranding as Meta, an effort by the leading social media platform to maintain a competitive edge in the changing landscape.

Numerous studies have since projected a promising future for the metaverse, with Gartner forecasting that one in four people globally will spend at least one hour a day in a metaverse for various activities by 2026. Similarly, McKinsey estimates that the metaverse could generate up to $5 trillion in value by 2030. As businesses grapple with the metaverse concept, many explore its potential and how it can effectively benefit their operations.

While 2021 is widely regarded as the beginning of the metaverse hype, the idea was coined in Neal Stephenson's 1992 science fiction novel *Snow Crash*. The novel depicts the metaverse as a virtual world where users can inhabit avatars and escape a dystopian reality. The metaverse is also visually portrayed in the 2018 Steven Spielberg film *Ready Player One*, which is based on a novel of the same name by Ernest Cline. The movie is set in 2045, when a significant portion of humanity utilizes the OASIS, a virtual reality simulation, to escape the real world.

The metaverse has roots in the gaming industry. Early depictions of a metaverse can be seen in games such as SimCity (first released in 1989) or Second Life (first released in 2003). Today, virtually all metaverse platforms available, including Roblox, Fortnite, The Sandbox, and Decentraland, are primarily gaming platforms featuring the ability to create in-game worlds as one of their key modes.

The origin of the prefix "meta" is Greek, and it denotes something that goes beyond or surpasses. Therefore, the current consensus is that the metaverse refers to a virtual realm transcending the physical world's limitations. However, it can also be viewed as a digital realm that closely mimics the physical world—including the interactions between digital replicas of humans and objects—which can be an alternative medium for marketers to interact with customers.

Metaverse is also built upon the idea of Web3—coined in 2014 by Ethereum co-founder Gavin Wood. He postulated Web3 as the next Internet iteration after Web1 and Web2. Web1 refers to the early stage of Internet development (1989–2004), where users only consumed content without the opportunity to be content creators themselves. We like to call it the Internet's product-centric era.

It changed in 2004 when the Internet was "reintroduced" as a platform for users to produce and share content. The start of this Web2 era was marked by the rise of platform companies such as Facebook (now Meta), Google, and

Amazon—each representing social media, search engines, and e-commerce platforms. It is the customer-centric version of the Internet.

The transition from Web1 to Web2 is about user empowerment, the overarching goal of Internet development that Web3 aims to continue (see Figure 7.1). Web3 supporters argue that in Web2, despite users being active creators, most content will still be owned and controlled by platform companies. Instead, they envision a future, decentralized Internet without the middlemen, where content creators and customers are directly and securely connected through blockchain. As a result, users can create, own, and even sell content and digital assets and have better control over their data. It also reduces inefficiencies inherent in the current platform economy. This is the human-centric version of the Internet.

Currently, two types of metaverse exist (see Figure 7.2). The first is the decentralized metaverse, which includes platforms such as The Sandbox, Decentraland, Axie Infinity, and Upland. The second type is the centralized metaverse, which consists of platforms such as Roblox, Fortnite, Minecraft, Second Life, and Horizon Worlds. The distinction between these types is based on the governance structure of the metaverse. Decentralized metaverses are governed by a community of users, while centralized metaverses are governed by a single entity, typically the company that develops them.

Decentralized metaverses are often regarded as the epitome of Web3, which is defined as a decentralized version of the Internet where power does not rest solely with large

THE MORE EMPOWERING INTERNET

HUMAN-CENTRIC (FUTURE)

- Blockchain-based decentralization
- Users own their content
- Communities control published content

CUSTOMER-CENTRIC (2004-NOW)

- Platform business model
- Users create and share content
- Platforms control and own content

PRODUCT-CENTRIC (1989-2004)

- Publishers created static content
- Users could only consume content

USER EMPOWERMENT

FIGURE 7.1 The Evolution of the Internet.

DECENTRALIZED VS. CENTRALIZED METAVERSE

DECENTRALIZED METAVERSE

- Governed by a community of users in a decentralized autonomous organization (DAO)
- Powered by blockchain technology
- Examples: The Sandbox, Decentraland, Axie Infinity, and Upland

CENTRALIZED METAVERSE

- Governed by a single entity, typically the platform companies
- Powered by platforms
- Examples: Roblox, Fortnite, Minecraft, Second Life, and Horizon Worlds

FIGURE 7.2 The Two Types of Metaverse.

platform companies but is distributed among the community of users. Therefore, the decentralized type can be classified as the Web3 metaverse, while the centralized type can be seen as the Web2 metaverse.

Toward the end of 2022, decentralized metaverses experienced a decline in popularity after an initial surge earlier in the year. Axie Infinity, for example, had 400,000 daily active users at the end of 2022, down from two million at the beginning of the year. This was partly due to the crypto-currency and non-fungible token (NFT) crashes in the same year, which raised doubts about decentralized blockchain technology.

Despite this decline, decentralized metaverses have introduced fresh innovations, albeit still controversial, to the gaming industry through blockchain technology. One example is Axie Infinity's "play-to-earn" model, where players can purchase NFTs of virtual monsters and battle them with others. The winners are then rewarded with cryptocurrency that they can exchange for money.

Another notable innovation in the decentralized metaverse is the creator economy, powered by cryptocurrencies and NFT certificates. In platforms such as Decentraland, users can buy and sell virtual lands, while in The Sandbox, they can create games and charge other users to play them. These innovations provide new ways for creators to monetize their work and for users to engage in the metaverse economy.

Centralized metaverses have shown resilience in contrast to the waning popularity of their decentralized counterparts. For example, the most recent statistics show that Roblox, Minecraft, and Fortnite have 214 million, 178 million, and 80 million monthly active users, respectively.

In addition, according to Metaversed (a metaverse consulting company), the average age of users in these centralized metaverses is 12–13 years old, with over 83 percent under 18. This also partially clarifies why decentralized metaverses are less popular than centralized ones, as the minimum legal age to establish a cryptocurrency wallet is 18. However, as these metaverse natives grow older and these platforms improve, they may shift toward decentralized options.

Essentially, the metaverse serves as a preferred social media format for Generation Alpha and the younger sub-set of Generation Z. This explains why many brands across categories, from entertainment, fashion, food and bever-age, and sports, to financial services, are tapping into the metaverse to target this youth segment with their offerings.

For instance, the 2022 MTV Video Music Awards included the "best metaverse performance" category fea-turing nominees who performed at concerts on Roblox and Fortnite. Footwear brands are tapping into the metaverse experience by offering virtual shoe inventories as customi-zation options for user avatars. Puma's virtual shoes are available on Meta, while Crocs can be found in Minecraft. Fidelity, a financial service company, is also educating young people about investing through a game on Roblox and Decentraland.

Essential Components of a Metaverse

A fully functioning metaverse has five essential components (see Figure 7.3). Firstly, every metaverse has *virtual assets,* which include a virtual environment and virtual objects. Secondly, *avatars* serve as digital representations of users within the metaverse, allowing them to participate in various experiences. Thirdly, the *user experience* within the metaverse determines how virtual assets and avatars interact. Fourthly,

WHAT'S INSIDE A METAVERSE

digital representations
of users

a virtual environment
and virtual objects

how virtual assets and
avatars interact

rules and guidelines
for development

how users create, buy,
and sell virtual assets

FIGURE 7.3   The Essential Components of a Metaverse.

a creator economy is necessary for users to create, buy, and sell digital assets. Lastly, every metaverse must have a *governance* structure to establish rules and oversee the development of various aspects of the metaverse.

Virtual Assets

What makes the metaverse immersive is that it is built on virtual environments. They are typically 3D places, ranging from platform-wide game worlds to social spaces and virtual marketplaces. They can be considered virtual equivalents of physical retail spaces, customer experience centers, or brand activation venues.

Brands recognize the potential of the metaverse as a space where younger customers will spend a significant amount of time and are thus investing in creating virtual environments. This involves purchasing virtual land within the metaverse, such as PwC Hong Kong and Adidas acquiring a plot in The Sandbox. Other brands are going even further by creating sub-worlds within larger metaverse platforms, such as Nikeland and Walmart Land within Roblox or Wendyverse within Horizon Worlds.

However, virtual stores are possibly the most valuable assets for brands and marketers in the metaverse, as they mirror the strategies businesses have been employing in the physical world to enhance customer experience and boost sales. Notable examples include the Gucci Vault, a high-end concept store in The Sandbox, and Samsung 837X in Decentraland, an immersive space modeled after the brand's flagship New York store.

These virtual stores represent the convergence of the metaverse and retail, offering a more immersive way for brands to showcase and sell their products online, compared to typical two-dimensional e-commerce websites. Customers can browse virtual store aisles in 3D and discover products like in a brick-and-mortar store.

The metaverse also offers an exciting potential for marketers to innovate their brand activations, from virtual concerts to visual fashion shows, and thereby engage younger demographics. Hyundai's activation in Roblox is an excellent illustration of this. The car manufacturer launched a brand activation in the metaverse called Hyundai Mobility Adventure, which showcases virtual spaces such as Festival Square, Future Mobility City, Eco-Forest, Racing Park, and Smart Tech Campus.

The metaverse offers more than just virtual spaces; it also features collectible virtual products that users can purchase, own, and even resell. This is especially possible in decentralized metaverses, where digital assets can be "tokenized," or recorded on the blockchain as NFTs. This presents a unique chance for brands to create digital replicas of their real-life products, which metaverse users can incorporate into their virtual experiences, from virtual sneakers to virtual sports cars.

Avatars

In the Internet era, digital identities have become widely established, with users frequently using relatively static usernames and profile pictures to represent themselves across various platforms such as social media and messaging apps.

Social media has enabled users to make their online identities more dynamic by frequently updating them through status updates and personal posts, offering a means to showcase their evolving personalities and styles. The concept of digital identities has been taken to a new level with the advent of the metaverse, where users establish their digital persona through what is known as an avatar.

An avatar is a visual representation of a user that serves as their identity within the virtual world. Think of it as the inhabitants in the metaverse that users can control. It enables users to navigate the virtual environment, interact with other users, and utilize digital assets.

Users can customize their avatars to represent their preferred facial and physical features, as well as their makeup, apparel, and accessories choices. This level of customization empowers users to express themselves and deepen immersion as they play in the metaverse.

It also presents opportunities for big brands and independent designers to create customization options. For instance, Maybelline and L'Oréal Professionnel have collaborated with the avatar creation platform Ready Player Me to offer users a selection of five makeup looks and trendy hairstyles within the metaverse. Fashion brands like Nike and Gucci also set up outfit personalization in the metaverse.

In addition to serving as a manifestation of users in the metaverse, avatars can also play the role of virtual influencers. For example, Maisie Williams, an actress who recently became H&M's Global Sustainability Ambassador, has been transformed into a digital avatar and will interact with shoppers in the virtual and real world. Similarly, the app start-up

Genies has launched the Avatar Agency, which creates digital versions of its celebrity clients, including DJ Khaled and Marshmello, and identifies brand ambassador opportunities for them.

The rapid advancement of AI has made it possible for virtual influencer avatars even to be fictional characters, as demonstrated by the success of FN Meka, an American virtual rapper with over one billion views on TikTok, and Lu do Magalu, the most popular virtual influencer with over 30 million followers across multiple social media platforms. In both the metaverse and the real world, brands may integrate virtual influencers into their marketing strategies and tap into their large fan base.

User Experience

The level of immersion in the metaverse depends heavily on user experience, as it guides the interaction between digital objects and avatars. The distinctive features of the metaverse dictate the basic requirements for user experience. At its core, the metaverse is a dynamic virtual environment that is constantly changing. Digital objects within the metaverse are not static, as users can interact with and transform them.

Another critical aspect of the metaverse is that it should resemble the real world to provide an intuitive user experience. While avatars can take on nonhuman forms and digital objects can have futuristic designs, there must be an element of familiarity, with avatar movements mirroring those of humans and object behaviors resembling their real-life counterparts. This way, users can navigate the world effortlessly and know how to perform tasks such as entering a building or using tools within the metaverse.

The metaverse is also a shared social experience where consistency and interactivity are crucial. For example, when a hundred people enter the metaverse simultaneously and engage in the same activity, the experience should be consistent from each person's perspective. Additionally, users must be able to interact with each other within the same metaverse.

These user experience characteristics of the metaverse can be illustrated by Marshmello's live virtual concert in Fortnite, where every movement was rendered into the virtual world in real time. The concert was designed to mimic Marshmello's real-life shows, with turntables on stage, visual attractions, and dancing audiences. Despite having 10 million concurrent attendees for the concert, Fortnite typically divides its gameplay into groups of 100 players, ensuring that every user experiences the same concert ambiance as the other 99 users.

To ensure that users stay engaged and motivated in the metaverse, it is also essential to incorporate gamification mechanics, including goals, achievements, and incentives. This strategy can help users maintain a sense of purpose and drive them to work together to achieve tasks woven into a compelling storyline. As users complete goals and attain achievements, the next phase of the narrative is unlocked, which keeps them immersed and engaged in the experience.

Starbucks Odyssey is an excellent example of using gamification as a key aspect of user experience. It is a newly launched blockchain-based membership program modeled after the Starbucks loyalty program, where customers collect points and earn rewards. It encourages members to complete a series of interactive games and immersive challenges called "journeys" to earn NFT-based collectible "journey stamps." As an incentive, members can get immersive physical-digital experiences like virtual coffee-making classes, special events at Starbucks Reserve Roasteries, or trips to the Starbucks coffee farm in Costa Rica.

This modified "play-to-earn" model of the decentralized metaverse further motivates users by allowing them to earn rewards through gameplay, which incentivizes them to keep returning to the metaverse and stay engaged.

Creator Economy

The metaverse's primary attractions will be the abundance of digital content and experiences, and content creators will play a crucial role in producing them. Users also function as creators and are highly motivated, given their ability to generate content and experiences or modify existing ones. Indeed, like social media, the metaverse presents an opportunity for a thriving ecosystem of content creators and service providers, including brands, online merchants, game designers, digital artists, and influencers, to leverage the platform to generate revenue.

One key factor that enables this creator economy is the presence of marketplaces available within most virtual worlds. These marketplaces serve as platforms for users to trade digital assets, including virtual real estate, avatar customization items, and other digital objects. Transactions within these marketplaces are often made with real money, which is then converted to the in-game currency in centralized metaverses or cryptocurrency in decentralized metaverses.

Blockchain technology facilitates the creator economy in a decentralized metaverse, with content creators being required to create non-fungible tokens (NFTs) for their digital assets to participate in trading within the virtual world. NFTs serve as unique certificates of ownership for digital objects, enabling secure trading and royalty payment for asset resale. While centralized metaverses offer similar opportunities, creators have less control and ownership over their work in centralized metaverses.

Nike's acquisition of RTFKT, a custom NFT sneaker designer, is an excellent example of NFT market potential. With this acquisition, Nike has generated $185 million from the metaverse marketplace in 2022, including royalties for the resale market. Unlike in real life, where revenue is generated only from primary sales, Nike can earn income from primary and secondary sales in the metaverse.

In addition to digital assets, creators can craft well-designed experiences in the metaverse. One of the unique features of the metaverse is its capacity for creators to construct virtual venues where their communities can connect, socialize, and interact with the creator directly. For instance, the tequila brand Patrón hosted a summer pop-up in Decentraland, where users could participate in quests to win a real-life trip.

Similarly, Walmart has established two metaverse spaces in Roblox—Walmart Land and Walmart's Universe of Play—which offer interactive experiences, virtual concerts, and a platform for brands sold at Walmart to showcase virtual merchandise. This immersive experience presents another monetization opportunity for the metaverse to become a new medium for advertising and brand activation.

The creator economy within the metaverse offers businesses a lucrative opportunity to generate revenue. Companies can partner with creators to develop and sell branded digital assets while also establishing marketplaces for asset trading. Moreover, businesses can create immersive experiences and virtual venues within the metaverse without the need for in-house development efforts.

Governance

The governance structure of a metaverse determines whether it is centralized or decentralized. In a centralized metaverse, the company that created the platform creates the rules and makes all the decisions, much like social media. For instance, Meta controls Horizon Worlds, and Epic Games manages Fortnite.

In some cases, an independent party may review the decision making of the platform owner. For instance, Meta has established the Oversight Board, an independent group of experts that reviews important decisions, particularly those related to content moderation. This ensures that Meta is not the sole entity responsible for making content moderation decisions.

Initially, Meta appoints the board members, but once their first terms are completed, the Oversight Board will take full responsibility for selecting all future members.

To ensure the board's independence, Meta has also established a trust to cover the operational costs associated with the board.

The governance structure in a decentralized metaverse is more intricate. One emerging governance model is the decentralized autonomous organization (DAO), which has no central governing body or a single corporate leader. Instead, power is distributed among its members, who make decisions together. A DAO operates similarly to a cooperative as it is collectively owned but uses blockchain technology to facilitate its operations.

The members of a DAO own crypto tokens—which function similarly to stocks in a company—and they are responsible for running the organization. The decision-making process in a DAO is bottom-up, with members working toward a common goal to benefit the organization. Proposals and voting govern every operational and financial decision to ensure all members have a voice. The blockchain allows for complete transparency of all decisions, and no single member can access the DAO's treasury without the members' approval.

In several instances, founders and investors of metaverse platforms are allocated a significant portion of tokens, granting them majority control over decision making. To mitigate this, certain metaverses have chosen to distribute governance tokens equitably among platform users. The immutable ownership and transparent transfer of these tokens help ensure that decision-making power remains in the hands of the entire community.

The popularity of the DAO goes beyond governance in the metaverse. The unique organization model of DAO is considered a Web3 alternative to the traditional corporate structure. According to DeepDAO, the DAO model is experiencing rapid growth, with over 12,000 DAOs currently in existence. These DAOs manage a collective fund of $23 billion and involve more than two million proposal makers and active voters as of May 2023.

DAOs can revolutionize how communities of customers engage with brands and participate in co-creating virtual products. It is also a new way for metaverse natives to invest their money toward shared goals. Customers can pool their funds together to create a DAO, partner with brands operating in the metaverse, and manage the direction of the partnership. A recent report by Long Dash consultancy found that 63 percent of Generation Z and Generation Y want more influence over brand decision making and, thus, are interested in participating in DAOs.

In response, some brands have partnered with and created DAOs to expose their customers to the metaverse environment. For example, Bud Light has collaborated with the Nouns DAO to showcase the first NFT and DAO in a Super Bowl commercial. The 45-second advertisement narrates four stories that illustrate the possibilities of challenging traditional norms, such as attending a concert in the Metaverse or exploring NFT art communities. In addition, the ads introduce Bud Light Next, a zero-carb beer, to a younger demographic, expanding the brand's customer base.

Another example is the NYX brand by L'Oréal, which has created its own DAO called GOJRS for beauty-focused virtual avatar creators. This DAO acts as an online beauty incubator, supporting creators in developing and monetizing digital avatar makeup. To ensure the independence of the DAO, non-transferable tokens will be utilized for voting on different projects. The DAO only includes four NYX executives, each holding a 2 percent share of the tokens. As DAO members have a say in the decision making, they become true advocates of the brands.

What's Next for the Metaverse?

The metaverse is a controversial topic for a reason. The skepticism is not directed toward the virtual worlds themselves, as they have existed for many decades in the form of world-building games. Even the oldest age groups can understand why it appeals to the younger generations. The root of the issue lies in the concept of Web3 and the blockchain technology that powers the decentralized version of it.

For Web3 enthusiasts, the vision of the metaverse is for a completely decentralized world without intermediaries where the power lies in the hands of the users. This idea is highly disruptive and could potentially signal the demise of the platform business model that has been prevalent since the early 2000s.

The platform business model is based on the idea that the power lies in connecting two parties, such as buyers and sellers, or content creators and consumers. This approach has disrupted various industries, with companies such as Amazon, Netflix, Uber, Airbnb, Android, Google, and Meta serving as examples of platforms that have disrupted traditional businesses in their respective sectors.

Web3 aims to disrupt these disruptors, which is an ambitious goal. Moreover, some hardcore supporters of Web3 not only intend to bring down platform companies but also more traditional intermediaries such as central banks through cryptocurrency technology. This renders Web3, and consequently the metaverse, a controversial subject.

It should be noted that the metaverse is still in its early stages of development and may not reach its full potential in the next decade. The end-game metaverse is an interoperable universe without platform owners. However, the current metaverse developers, particularly those in centralized platforms, are primarily the platform companies themselves who invest heavily to avoid obsolescence. Consequently, each version of the metaverse remains a closed ecosystem with unique assets and currency, lacking interoperability. Users who wish to explore different metaverses are required to register separately for each one and cannot utilize their existing virtual identity across multiple metaverses.

In addition, blockchain technology remains a complicated and divisive subject for most customers, particularly after the cryptocurrency and NFT crashes and Meta's decline in market value in 2022. While customers may desire the benefits of a blockchain-based metaverse, they oppose the complexities and controversies associated with blockchain technology, such as setting up cryptocurrency wallets or purchasing NFTs.

Therefore, businesses must make this experience as frictionless as possible for average customers who are not Web3 enthusiasts. For instance, blockchain-powered Starbucks Odyssey uses the term "journey stamps" instead of NFTs.

Furthermore, it enables members to purchase these stamps directly with their credit cards, eliminating the need for cryptocurrency.

Despite this less-than-ideal scenario, businesses can still benefit from this new evolution. This intermediate milestone—Web2.5—is necessary to advance toward the ultimate customer empowerment that Web3 envisions. Web 2.5 seeks to combine the familiarity of Web2 with the decentralized technology of Web3. An instance of Web 2.5 is demonstrated by Starbucks Odyssey incorporating Web3 technology seamlessly into its existing loyalty program mechanism. This integration ensures that Starbucks customers can enjoy the benefits of blockchain technology without being overwhelmed by its complexity.

Summary: The Future Form of Social Media Platforms

The metaverse is an immersive virtual world that closely resembles the physical world and is considered the next step in the evolution of the Internet, or Web3. A fully functioning metaverse has five essential components: virtual assets, avatars, user experience, creator economy, and governance. As it is the preferred social media format for Generation Z and Generation Alpha, marketers can use the metaverse as an alternative way to interact with customers.

There are two types of metaverses: decentralized and centralized. Decentralized metaverses are governed by a community of users connected through blockchain technology, while centralized metaverses are governed by a single entity. Although skepticism still exists, particularly regarding the decentralized metaverse, it can transform how businesses deliver immersive customer experiences.

REFLECTION QUESTIONS

- How can you make use of the metaverse for marketing? What specific strategies or ideas would apply to your industry sector or company?

- How can businesses ensure that their use of the metaverse for marketing is ethical and does not cause the same issues observed with social media?

PART III

The Marketing 6.0 Experience

CHAPTER 8

Multisensory Marketing

Delivering Immersive Experiences for the Five Senses

The Internet has permeated every aspect of our lives, from work to home and everything in between. The pandemic has further exacerbated this, with people being compelled to stay and work from home, blurring the boundaries of working hours. Workers were forced to have more online meetings that were typically more intense and demanding for human cognitive ability.

According to a recent study conducted by Meltwater and We Are Social, the average global daily Internet usage exceeds 6.5 hours across all devices. This figure is closer to 7 hours per day in the United States. On the one hand, this surge in Internet usage has created more opportunities to connect with customers through digital channels. But on the other hand, it has also introduced a troubling phenomenon known as digital fatigue.

Digital fatigue is the physical and mental exhaustion that arises from excessive and prolonged use of Internet-connected devices. According to a report by Deloitte, one in three people felt overwhelmed with technology and exhibited signs of digital fatigue. This issue is of great concern as it can result in a decline in workplace productivity and potentially lead to more severe mental health problems.

In response to this growing problem, emerging trends have surfaced among younger generations to combat digital fatigue (see Figure 8.1). One such trend is the "digital detox," where people limit their screen time by taking breaks from the Internet and digital devices. Instead, they meet friends in person and make meaningful connections at a "third place," like a coffee shop. Brands are tapping into this trend. Apple, for example, encourages people to monitor and limit their screen time. Likewise, Heineken launched a campaign

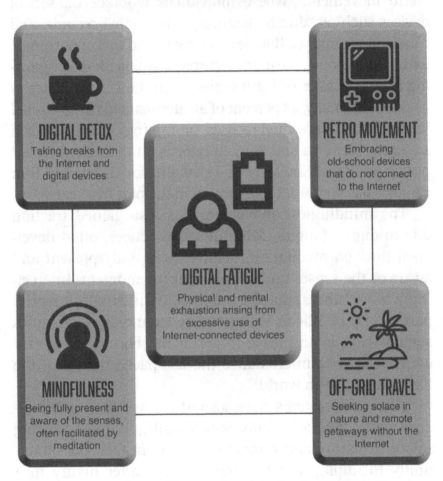

FIGURE 8.1   Emerging Multisensory Trends to Combat Digital Fatigue.

promoting less screen time and more socializing with friends over a drink.

Another popular trend among younger generations is the "retro movement," where individuals embrace old-school devices such as "dumb" feature phones, vinyl records, and classic film cameras. Businesses have seized this opportunity, with HMD Global, the manufacturer of Nokia phones, reporting increased sales of feature phones in the United States in 2022. Additionally, 43 percent of all albums sold in the United States in 2022 were vinyl records, prompting companies such as Audio-Technica and Sony to refocus on their vinyl record player products. Similarly, the demand for disposable film cameras has seen a 3.3-fold growth in the past five years.

The mindfulness movement has also gained traction due to digital fatigue. Mindfulness practices, often developed through meditation, involve being fully present and aware of the senses and emotions at the moment. Interestingly, mindfulness gained popularity in the corporate world, particularly in Silicon Valley, where technology companies such as Google and Meta reside. It has become a tool for employees to counterbalance the fast-paced nature of the technology-driven world.

Young generations have also attempted to counterbalance digital fatigue by embarking on off-grid travel, seeking solace in nature and remote getaways. In fact, the opportunity to unplug has become a sought-after luxury in a world where digital technology constantly surrounds us. As a result, platforms such as Airbnb now offer search filters for people seeking off-the-grid accommodations and other nature-focused options such as camping, countryside retreats, cabins, and national parks.

Marketers are partly responsible for digital fatigue by fueling the proliferation of digital media. Mass-distributed content lacking personalization can overwhelm customers with irrelevant spam, frustrating them when searching for valuable information. But marketers can also be part of the solution by embracing the concept of multisensory marketing.

Multisensory marketing engages multiple human senses to evoke positive emotions and influence behaviors. Unlike digital content and experiences primarily focusing on sight and sound, multisensory marketing strives to balance stimuli across all five senses. The trends of digital detox, going retro, mindfulness, and off-grid travel are all forms of multisensory marketing. Spending time in a multisensory environment has been shown to improve attention and increase happiness. It is also an essential pillar of delivering immersive customer experiences.

Engaging the Five Senses

The five senses act as various sensors that transmit messages to the human brain, shaping perceptions of the environment and influencing decision making. The senses—sight, sound, smell, touch, and taste—indeed provide unique and subconscious channels into customers' minds (see Figure 8.2). Marketers can utilize these channels to break through the clutter of massive content competing for attention. They can build positive perceptions and position their brands in customers' minds. Moreover, the multisensory approach has been proven to enhance and deepen the customer experience by setting the mood. Ultimately, this approach can

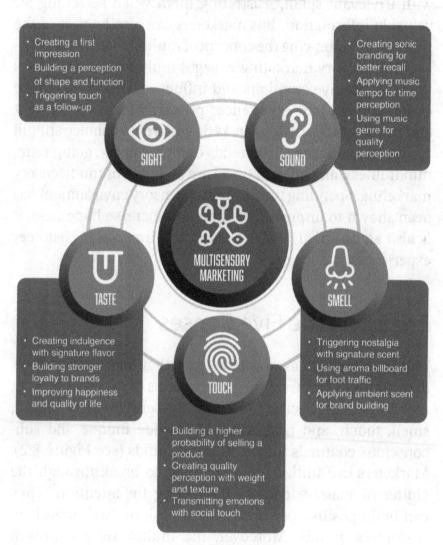

ENGAGING
THE FIVE SENSES

SIGHT
- Creating a first impression
- Building a perception of shape and function
- Triggering touch as a follow-up

SOUND
- Creating sonic branding for better recall
- Applying music tempo for time perception
- Using music genre for quality perception

MULTISENSORY MARKETING

TASTE
- Creating indulgence with signature flavor
- Building stronger loyalty to brands
- Improving happiness and quality of life

SMELL
- Triggering nostalgia with signature scent
- Using aroma billboard for foot traffic
- Applying ambient scent for brand building

TOUCH
- Building a higher probability of selling a product
- Creating quality perception with weight and texture
- Transmitting emotions with social touch

FIGURE 8.2   Multisensory Marketing Approach.

influence customer behavior, making it a powerful tool for driving purchases.

Companies such as Starbucks are recognized for implementing a multisensory approach in their marketing strategies. Their stores feature visually appealing decorations and soothing ambient music as consistent elements. However, as a coffee shop chain, Starbucks emphasizes engaging the senses of smell and taste.

Its aroma of coffee is often described as "heady, rich, full-bodied, and suggestive," perfectly complementing the coffee-drinking experience. Starbucks has long been known for safeguarding this signature scent, enforcing policies such as no indoor smoking and no strong perfumes for baristas. They have even tailored their food menu to avoid strongly scented items that could compete with or overpower the coffee aroma.

Each of the five human senses serves a distinct purpose in shaping human behavior. Consequently, comprehending how each sense responds to stimuli enables marketers to incorporate appropriate multisensory elements into their immersive experience designs. Moreover, since the human brain perceives stimuli as a unified experience, marketers must discover the perfect combination of ingredients to deliver a coherent and ultimately immersive sensation.

The Sight

Vision is the most dominant sensory modality that shapes perception and cognition in the human brain. Neuroscientists and researchers have estimated that approximately

80 percent of the information processed by the brain is acquired through sight. Consequently, a significant portion of the human brain is dedicated to processing visual information, whereas processing stimuli from other senses occurs in comparatively smaller brain regions.

This understanding helps shed light on the addictive nature of visual stimuli, such as screen dependence seen in younger generations. Spending hours on smartphones chatting with friends, using social media, streaming content, and playing video games is a manifestation of this addiction.

Given the importance of vision, it is no surprise that most people (70 percent) express a higher fear when faced with the prospect of losing sight. In contrast, the fear of losing other senses typically ranges from 2 to 7 percent, as evidenced by a YouGov poll. This disparity can be attributed to the significant role vision plays in daily human activities such as driving cars, working with computers, watching television, and reading books.

Furthermore, human eyes possess remarkable processing speed, especially regarding images. Research conducted at the Massachusetts Institute of Technology has revealed that humans can process visual information in as little as 13 milliseconds. This finding explains why visual cues in advertising have a more profound impact on customer response than text-based content.

A notable example of this phenomenon is Mastercard's logo redesign, where the company simply removed the brand name while retaining its iconic interlocking red and yellow circles. The company reported that 80 percent of people can still recognize the brand upon seeing the logo without the accompanying name.

In the field of marketing, captivating the sense of sight holds significant value across the customer journey. Visual stimuli frequently shape the first impression of products and services. For example, upon entering retail stores, customers often form their first impressions based on visual cues, including the store's façade, logo, and overall decor. While perusing the aisles, customers intuitively observe product packaging, paying attention to its form, color, and imagery.

The evaluation of shape, whether it pertains to physical objects or products, significantly influences the perception of their intended function. A compelling example is the round shape of Starbucks tables, which encourages interaction among people as it exudes a more inviting atmosphere than square tables. Consequently, the presence of round tables cultivates a perception of a social environment, alleviating feelings of loneliness for customers occupying that space.

Vision also serves as a catalyst for customers to engage in tactile experiences. When customers are captivated by visual stimuli, their natural inclination is to explore products through touch. This tactile interaction, in turn, increases the likelihood of a purchase. Apple effectively applies this principle in its approach to selling MacBook products.

The MacBook laptop screens displayed in Apple Stores are intentionally positioned at a precise angle of 76 degrees. This deliberate angle tempts customers to instinctively adjust the screen's position, enticing them to touch and explore the product further. By creating this interactive experience, Apple effectively capitalizes on the connection between visual engagement and the subsequent desire to engage with the product.

This principle is widely implemented in the consumer packaged goods industry, where products often showcase playful colors and bold fonts on their packaging to entice customers to pick them off the shelves. For example, two prominent beverage brands, Pepsi and Fanta, have undergone significant visual identity redesign to foster more vibrant and playful perceptions.

Fanta introduced a major logo redesign and incorporated new, lively colors and artwork on its packaging. This fresh approach aims to capture attention and create a sense of fun and excitement for consumers. Similarly, Pepsi unveiled an enhanced logo featuring an electric blue and black color scheme, evoking a sense of boldness and confidence in its brand image.

The power of visuals makes them a favorite stimulus for businesses to engage with customers, primarily through TV, print, and digital media. However, this abundance of visual content also creates a problem, leading to clutter and sensory overload.

The Sound

The sense of hearing—or the auditory modality—holds the second highest dominance among the five senses. It contributes about 10 percent of the total information the human brain receives and processes. Together, visual stimuli (80 percent) and auditory stimuli (10 percent) significantly shape human perceptions and decision making, accounting for about 90 percent of sensory experiences.

Unsurprisingly, digital content emphasizing audiovisual elements has become the dominant form of media in recent years. This is because the human response time to integrated audiovisual stimuli is faster when compared to information that is solely visual or auditory.

Social media users, for instance, have better comprehension when content is presented in audiovisuals rather than through static images or silent videos. Consequently, by incorporating sound narratives into visual content, marketers can effectively convey a message to their audience and enhance its impact.

Sound plays a crucial role in creating an immersive experience as it enriches the perception of space. Therefore, soundscape development focuses solely on shaping people's perception of space through the acoustic environment. Subconsciously, people can distinguish whether they are in an outdoor area, a concert hall, a crowded coffee shop, or a bathroom simply by perceiving the sounds they hear and how they are reflected in the surrounding spaces.

A notable example is the Nike Icon Studios in Los Angeles, where photographers and videographers create brand imaging content for Nike's global brand campaign. These studios meticulously consider the selection of materials for the flooring and ceiling to effectively control sound within the space, ensuring a high-quality acoustic environment.

Other examples include UK retailer Selfridges and the Swedish shopping mall Emporia, which have different visual designs and soundscapes for each section, personifying different product categories and audiences.

With these distinct thematic soundscapes, customers are fully aware of where they are, which helps them navigate the entire space.

The impact of sound on branding is also very significant. For example, sonic branding—the audio uniquely associated with a specific brand—has proven to be an effective tool. Sonic branding can be in the form of a "sound logo" (an audio representation of a brand logo), a jingle (a piece of short music that appear consistently in advertising), and a longer brand theme song.

Mastercard is an example of a brand that embraces sonic branding. As the payment processing company ventures into voice-controlled devices such as smart speakers and wearables, it recognizes the importance of having an audio format for its brand. To achieve this, Mastercard created a "sound logo," an audio rendition of its recognizable red and yellow logo. This 30-second lyric-less instrumental melody is integrated into every audiovisual marketing communication, and its short version plays after every successful credit card transaction at the point of sale.

However, Mastercard's sonic branding goes beyond a single melody. The sound has been adapted into various musical genres and versions across different regions. Additionally, Mastercard took a unique approach by developing a music album called "Priceless," available on Spotify.

This album features songs that subtly incorporate the sonic brand into pop music. It is important to note that the goal of this type of sonic branding is not solely to attract a massive listenership. Instead, it aims to create brand recognition and establish emotional connections with customers.

Sonic branding adds a powerful dimension to brand identities traditionally confined to visual applications.

Ambient sound also plays a role in guiding behaviors by shaping perception. One example is the influence of music tempo, which refers to the speed at which music progresses, typically measured in beats per minute. Music tempo can impact the perception of time, and marketers can leverage this effect to control shopping speed based on their objectives.

A faster music tempo tends to make customers shop quicker, while a slower tempo encourages a slower shopping experience. As a result, a fast tempo is often employed to induce impulsive shopping behaviors, which align well with low-priced and low-involvement products such as fast food and groceries. Conversely, a slower tempo is more suitable for higher-priced and high-involvement products such as jewelry and consumer electronics, where customers need more time to evaluate their options.

The choice of music genres can evoke specific perceptions of quality as different genres elicit particular emotional states. For example, jazz, with its rhythmic patterns and improvisation, has a soothing effect and creates a relaxing mood. Jazz embodies sophistication and style when used as ambient music, making it well suited for high-end galleries and boutiques.

In contrast, soul and R&B music emphasizes vocals accompanied by upbeat background music, exuding a warm and welcoming ambiance. This genre is particularly suitable for social venues such as bars and cafés, creating an inviting atmosphere for patrons. Finally, pop and electronic dance music, known for their energetic beats, create a playful ambiance fitting for fashion stores. The unique characteristics of these genres add a dynamic element to the shopping experience, enhancing the overall atmosphere.

The Smell

Given that sight and sound comprise 90 percent of the information processed in the human brain, each of the remaining three senses contributes only about 1 to 4 percent. Despite their lesser dominance, stimuli targeting these senses play a crucial role in alleviating the overwhelming burden on human vision and hearing, often leading to digital fatigue. Furthermore, actively engaging these three senses can set companies apart from their competitors, as many tend to focus heavily on the audiovisual aspects of the customer experience.

The sense of smell, triggered by scents, is essential for a multisensory experience. Unlike audiovisual stimuli, which can be effectively delivered in physical and digital spaces, scents are most effectively experienced in the physical realm. There is an emerging field known as digital olfaction that aims to mimic the human sense of smell and transmit specific scents digitally through devices such as diffusers or wires attached to the nostrils. However, using digital olfaction devices is currently uncomfortable, limiting the application of scents to physical experiences.

The most critical role of smell is to evoke feelings of nostalgia. This is because smell and memory are intricately connected, thanks to the brain's anatomy, which enables odor stimuli to go directly to the brain regions responsible for memory regulation. This phenomenon is often called the "Proust moment," where a sensory experience, typically triggered by a scent, brings forth a vivid memory from the distant past in people's minds.

So while audiovisual stimuli are effective in the short run, olfactory stimuli have a lasting effect. Marketers in the scent-related industries have leveraged this approach for many years. For example, Maison Margiela's Replica fragrance line is inspired by memory-triggering smells such as the fireside, library, and beach. Nespresso, for instance, released a limited edition Festive Variations coffee that evokes the nostalgia of family Christmas time.

Another marketing application of scent is using aroma billboards, commonly employed by food service companies such as coffee shops and bakeries, to attract foot traffic. For example, stores such as Starbucks and Panera Bread deliberately design their coffee brewing and baking areas as open spaces to disperse the enticing aroma of their products to passersby, enticing them to enter the stores and make purchases.

Aroma billboards typically feature solid and bold smells carefully selected to diffuse outdoors and attract people. However, there are exceptions to this principle, particularly in non-food service spaces. For instance, apparel retailer Abercrombie & Fitch learned from their past experiences when developing their signature scent to attract people into their stores. Initially, their overpowering "Fierce" fragrance had a negative impact, driving customers away from the stores. In response, Abercrombie & Fitch opted for a more subtle and welcoming scent called "Ellwood."

Companies also utilize ambient scents to create specific associations with their brands. Hotels, in particular, are known for adopting signature scents that embody their unique hotel characteristics. For instance, Westin, which emphasizes wellness amenities, utilizes a smell called "White Tea," which revitalizes and energizes guests.

On the other hand, W Hotels, positioning itself as a modern establishment with provocative designs and extravagant lifestyles, employs the scent "Citron No.5" to showcase the vibrant personality of the brand. These scents not only enhance the ambiance but also contribute to a cohesive narrative that aligns with the brand values.

The Touch

In contrast to the other senses, touch does not have a dedicated organ within the human body. While the skin is commonly associated with touch, it comprises numerous individual sensory nerves that collaborate to generate the sensation of touch. Through the sense of touch, humans can distinguish various physical characteristics of objects, such as their shape, texture, hardness, weight, and temperature.

Technological advancements have successfully brought the sensation of touch to the digital realm. For example, digital interfaces such as mobile phone touch screens, laptop touchpads, and gaming console joysticks provide users tactile feedback, enhancing their experience in operating these devices. As a result, it becomes feasible to incorporate touch as a multisensory experience in digital environments such as the metaverse.

Another noteworthy aspect of touch is its combination of passive and active sensing. Individuals are not mere recipients of touch stimuli; they actively engage in touching objects to explore their qualities. This active involvement is a significant factor in why customers are more inclined to purchase products when they have the freedom to touch and interact with them firsthand. Furthermore, tactile experiences increase willingness to pay as customers feel they can better assess the product value.

This phenomenon is closely tied to a concept in psychology known as the "endowment effect." According to this concept, people tend to assign more value to items they already own and are more inclined to keep them. When customers physically touch and try products, it creates a sense of ownership, increasing the likelihood that they will maintain this feeling by making a purchase.

This is especially important for high-involvement products that require customer exploration before purchase. Therefore, retailers such as Apple Store and Best Buy actively encourage customers to engage with their products in-store. Similar tactics can be observed in car dealerships and apparel stores, where test drives and fitting rooms facilitate sales by granting potential buyers a sensation of product ownership.

Tactile perception also plays a role in shaping customers' perception of quality. For example, readers may perceive a magazine or book that feels heavy and uses textured papers as more premium. On the other hand, the lightweight and smoothness of aluminum materials in smartphones can contribute to a sense of premium quality for buyers. Similarly, coffee drinkers often opt for ceramic mugs over paper cups, as they believe that ceramic mugs better retain the taste of the coffee. Depending on the specific attribute that customers value, the tactile experience can effectively deliver it, further shaping their perception of a product's quality.

However, one of the most vital functions of touch lies in its ability to convey emotions. A study led by Matthew Hertenstein uncovered that person-to-person touch, when applied to any appropriate part of the body, can effectively transmit eight distinct emotions: anger, fear, happiness, sadness, disgust, love, gratitude, and sympathy. For instance, a firm hold or squeeze without movement is often interpreted as conveying fear, while gentle holding, patting, and rubbing are commonly associated with communicating sympathy. The research found the accuracy levels of these emotional transmissions range from 50 to 78 percent.

The implications of this finding on in-person customer experiences are profound, as the frontline staff can convey emotions to customers not only through facial expressions and voice tones but also through appropriate forms of contact, such as handshakes. Touch can serve as an additional channel for effectively communicating with customers and humanizing the experience.

The Taste

In a narrow definition, taste refers to the sensation perceived by humans on their tongues, typically encompassing sweet, sour, salty, bitter, and umami (commonly known as savory). However, the sense of taste is more complex, as it intertwines with the other four senses to form what we know as "flavor."

The flavor is truly a multisensory experience. For example, an experiment at Oxford University has demonstrated that consuming yogurt with a lightweight plastic spoon enhances the perception of creaminess and adds a sense of luxury compared to using a heavy metal spoon. Additionally, the yogurt tastes sweeter when enjoyed with a light-colored spoon instead of a darker one.

Similarly, an experiment at Auckland University of Technology uncovered the influence of ambient music on the enjoyment of chocolate gelato. When stimulating food court music was played, people perceived a more pronounced bitterness in the taste. Conversely, when delightful café music played in the background, the sweetness of the gelato became more apparent and satisfying.

In addition to vision, audio, and tactile sensations, the sense of smell plays a significant role in shaping our perception of flavor. Approximately 80 percent of what humans perceive as taste is attributed to smell. This explains why people often perceive food as bland when their nasal passages are congested due to a common cold. Thus, flavor emerges as a complex integration of all five senses, culminating in the ultimate sensory experience.

Many brands have delved into the business of flavor sensations, even if their core focus lies outside the food and beverage industry. Take, for instance, Mastercard, a company renowned for its multisensory strategies. In addition to its existing multisensory ventures, Mastercard has expanded into the culinary domain, offering a complete five-sense engagement. Through its "Priceless" restaurants, the company aims to create immersive, multisensory experiences curated by famous chefs and mixologists.

The furniture retailer IKEA is another illustration of providing an indulgent culinary experience while selling the core products. Its restaurant offers signature Scandinavian meals such as the famous Swedish meatballs. The food business has become an effective way for IKEA to increase foot traffic as the company discovered that 30 percent of the store visitors came to get food, and some ended up shopping for furniture inside the stores. Furthermore, IKEA found that providing food halls extended the time spent in its stores, which helped sell the more expensive product lines.

The sense of taste is intricately tied to the concept of brand loyalty. Specific taste can become strongly associated with a particular brand, leaving a lasting impact that drives loyalty. A fascinating case study is that of New Coke. In 1985, New Coke was introduced in response to a blind taste test that revealed customers preferred the sweeter flavor of Pepsi. However, the customers' response was overwhelmingly negative to the new product as they had already formed a solid connection to the original taste associated with the Coca-Cola brand. Interestingly, during the blind taste test, customers did not favor Coca-Cola, but when the brand was attached to the same beverage, their preference shifted instantly.

However, the primary purpose of taste is to enhance happiness and improve the overall quality of life. It has long been recognized that good food and delightful flavors are closely linked to a higher quality of life. For instance, when patients cannot consume certain foods due to dietary restrictions caused by certain illnesses, their motivation and enjoyment often diminish. Furthermore, a recent study discovered that individuals who experienced anosmia, the loss of the sense of smell and taste due to contracting COVID-19, also suffered from increased levels of depression and anxiety. This highlights taste's vital role in enriching our lives and overall well-being.

The influence of taste on happiness can also be significantly attributed to the social nature of dining, where we gather and interact with friends and family. Recognizing this, many retailers incorporate restaurant spaces within their stores to offer this social experience. By combining the multisensory aspects of flavor with the communal dining atmosphere, businesses can elevate the overall customer experience to new heights, which are almost impossible to replicate in the digital realm.

Building Multisensory Experiences

Understanding how each sense influences customers' minds helps marketers explore the possibilities of engaging their customers with sensory experiences. Humans experience multisensory stimulation daily, and the human brain processes these stimuli as one unified experience. Thus, it becomes crucial to orchestrate these stimuli harmoniously, ensuring their congruence and intended impact when combined. Generally, three major stages are involved in creating multisensory experiences (see Figure 8.3).

Step 1: Determine the Key Objectives

The initial step involves determining the intended impact of the multisensory experience. There are essentially three objectives that marketers can achieve with a multisensory approach. Firstly, marketers can adopt a multisensory approach to developing brands by establishing associations

BUILDING MULTISENSORY EXPERIENCES

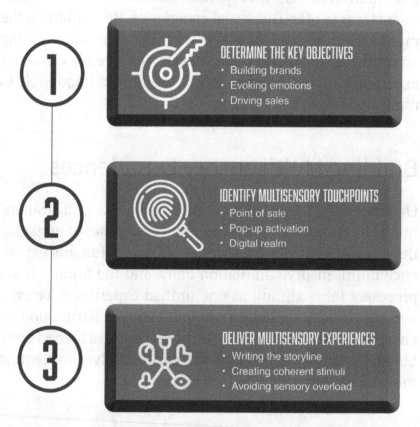

①

DETERMINE THE KEY OBJECTIVES
- Building brands
- Evoking emotions
- Driving sales

②

IDENTIFY MULTISENSORY TOUCHPOINTS
- Point of sale
- Pop-up activation
- Digital realm

③

DELIVER MULTISENSORY EXPERIENCES
- Writing the storyline
- Creating coherent stimuli
- Avoiding sensory overload

FIGURE 8.3   Three Steps of Multisensory Experience Design.

between brands and distinct sensory elements. For instance, brands can be linked to distinctive sounds, scents, and tastes, expanding brand recognition beyond key visuals.

Secondly, employing a multisensory approach is also valuable in eliciting desired emotions that brands aim for their customers to experience. This empowers brands to create an atmosphere that aligns with specific touchpoints between the brand and its customers. Ambient scent and music, for instance, can be tailored to induce relaxation or excitement, depending on the objectives.

Lastly, a multisensory approach is a powerful tool to drive sales by encouraging customer purchase action. Engaging multiple senses, particularly touch, in experiencing the product helps companies convince customers to buy it.

Step 2: Identify Multisensory Touchpoints

The next step involves identifying opportunities to apply multisensory cues throughout the customer journey. Brands must map the customer journey and determine the most appropriate points to incorporate sensory stimuli. Essentially, there are three significant touchpoints where brands can effectively deliver multisensory experiences.

Firstly, companies can implement sensory cues at the point of sale, which includes retail stores, restaurants, cafés, and other venues where transactions occur. These locations serve as the multisensory representation of the brand, allowing for immersive experiences.

Secondly, the multisensory approach can be applied to pop-up venues where brands conduct activation campaigns or temporary exhibitions. Unlike point-of-sale locations, pop-up spaces are often smaller and situated within larger spaces such as shopping malls or public areas. These venues are typically used to launch new products or introduce new campaigns, focusing on specific aspects of the brand offering.

Finally, multisensory experiences can also be extended to digital realms, although the cues are primarily limited to visual and auditory elements with a touch of tactile stimuli. Brands that have a presence in the metaverse engage customers with dynamic audiovisual components and often provide extensions to in-real-life (IRL) experiences.

Step 3: Deliver Multisensory Experiences

The final step involves delivering coherent and seamless multisensory stimuli within the overall customer experience. As described in this chapter, each sensory cue conveys specific messages about the unique product quality and brand values. To ensure coherence, it is essential to establish an umbrella story that aligns with the message brands wish to convey.

Once the story is in place, ensuring that all sensory cues are consistent with the narrative becomes crucial. Brands must strive for congruence among the stimuli, ensuring they do not contradict one another and that they evoke the same emotions and are associated with the same product features.

This approach is evident in Disney's theme park designs. Disney's theme parks aim to create magical worlds that bring beloved characters and stories from books and movies to life, offering guests an immersive experience that turns imagination into reality. Every attraction is meticulously designed with familiar storylines, plots, and characters. Moreover, guests are encouraged to interact with their favorite characters, who appear in parades, live shows, and meet-and-greets throughout the theme parks. Even the dining venues are themed restaurants where every dish is named after a beloved character.

However, it is vital to avoid sensory overload. In multi-sensory marketing, more stimuli do not necessarily result in a better customer experience. Overwhelming customers with a combination of stimuli may have a negative impact and drive them away from the brand. Often, the most successful cues are subtle and implicit. Finding the right formula is, therefore, pivotal.

Summary: Delivering Immersive Experiences for the Five Senses

The excessive use of the Internet and digital devices has led to digital fatigue. This fatigue is primarily caused by sensory overload, as the abundance of audiovisual content primarily targets only two major senses: vision and hearing. A multisensory marketing approach can address digital fatigue by engaging all five senses and counterbalancing the strain on specific senses. However, it is important to note that delivering a fully multisensory experience is primarily achievable in physical environments, with limited application to virtual realms where only a few sensory stimuli can be replicated.

Each sensory stimulus conveys specific messages to the audience, shaping brand personalities and product quality. Furthermore, each cue plays a distinct role in evoking emotions and driving purchase behavior. The key to successful multisensory marketing lies in coherently orchestrating these sensory stimuli.

REFLECTION QUESTIONS

- How can you incorporate multisensory elements into your product and customer experience? What innovative strategies do you have in mind to implement multisensory marketing within your company?
- Will digital technology catch up to enable a fully immersive multisensory customer experience in digital environments? If so, what steps can brands take to prevent the virtual experience from becoming overwhelming and exacerbating digital fatigue?

CHAPTER 9

Spatial Marketing

Delivering Natural Human-Machine Interactions

In the past, humans used various methods to interact with machines, such as buttons and switches. With the advent of personal computers, new means of interaction, such as a keyboard and a mouse, were introduced. Similarly, early smartphones utilized physical keyboards and styluses. However, in 2007, the first iPhone revolutionized the smartphone industry by popularizing touch screens as the primary interface. Touchscreens became commonplace in most smartphones shortly after, establishing an intuitive human-machine interface.

Today, screens have become the portals for people to transition between the physical and digital realms. People can now intuitively interact with screens on smartphones, tablets, self-service kiosks, automated teller machines, and vending machines. Even in social situations or physical spaces such as coffee shops, individuals often shift their attention to their phones, immersing themselves in the digital world.

The recent advancements in technology will further fuel these more natural human-machine interactions. We believe many advanced technologies are designed to imitate human abilities and behaviors so that machines can interact with humans better (see Figure 9.1). AI is a prime example of this, as it seeks to replicate human cognitive skills such as learning, problem-solving, and decision making. Moreover, natural language processing (NLP), a branch of AI, focuses on imitating human language interactions. This enables machines such as chatbots and voice assistants to understand and respond to written and spoken requests.

Sensors play a crucial role in mimicking human senses. Facial and image recognition technologies, for instance, aim to replicate human vision by enabling machines to identify

ADVANCED TECHNOLOGIES ARE BIONICS

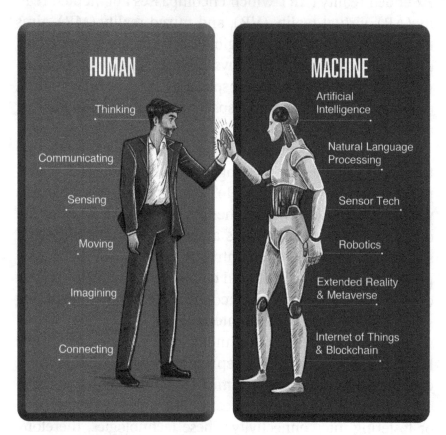

FIGURE 9.1 Human-Inspired Technologies.

and distinguish objects similarly to humans. Robotics also imitate human movements and actions, empowering robots to execute tasks such as walking, lifting, and climbing, thus assisting humans in physically demanding activities.

Human imagination, a distinct capability that enables comprehension of abstract concepts and ideas without physical form, has also inspired technological advancements. Extended reality (XR), which encompasses augmented reality (AR), virtual reality (VR), and mixed reality (MR), aims to replicate this human imagination by creating immersive experiences that blend the physical and digital worlds. Likewise, the metaverse is also inspired by human imagination, as it is an imaginative virtual space where people can interact and explore.

The inherently social nature of humans has also inspired technologies aimed at creating interconnectivity. For example, the Internet of Things (IoT) is a system that connects various devices and enables them to communicate and share data. This interconnectedness allows for more efficient and seamless automation and control of devices. Another example is blockchain, a distributed database that aims to create a decentralized network of interconnected computers, enabling secure transactions without intermediaries.

In essence, advanced technologies often seek to imitate human abilities, whether replicating cognitive functions, enabling communications, mimicking human senses, empowering physical movements, creating imaginative experiences, or fostering interconnectivity. These technologies, therefore, provide new possibilities for natural interaction between humans and humanlike machines involving voice commands, face recognition, and hand gestures.

An emerging field that can potentially leverage these technological advancements is spatial computing, which enables humans to interact with machines and digital content within a physical space. While screen-based interactions remain relevant, spatial computing offers more natural ways to engage with technology.

For example, the mere presence of a person can trigger devices to operate. This is evident in smart homes, where residents' presence can automatically adjust lighting and temperature without needing touchscreen controllers. Alternatively, residents can use preset voice commands or clap their hands to change the room's ambiance.

Advancements in spatial computing have further enhanced the convergence of physical and digital experiences. Imagine similar applications in retail experiences, where customers entering a store are detected by various sensors that prompt in-app notifications on their mobile phones. Facial recognition cameras can also identify the demographic profile of store visitors, leading to an LED wall lighting up and recommending personalized promotions for the day.

This type of experiential marketing is what we call spatial marketing, where marketers leverage spatial computing to introduce products and deliver promotions within an interactive physical environment. It allows marketers to add virtual 3D experiences onto physical space, allowing users to interact with environments that feature digital elements.

An excellent illustration of spatial marketing is Disney's recent patent for a virtual-world simulator for implementation in real-world venues such as theme parks, hotels, and cruise ships. This innovative technology enables Disney to monitor the movements of its guests and project multimedia content onto 3D surfaces and objects as guests approach them. As a result, visitors can engage with Disney characters in 3D holograms while exploring various theme park attractions. This cutting-edge technology can be categorized as augmented reality (AR) since it overlays digital content onto the real-world view. The key differentiator is that it operates without needing additional devices, providing a frictionless experience for the guests.

Spatial marketing combines the effectiveness of physical space with the rising appeal of digital interfaces. These blurred boundaries between physical and digital realms have created an entirely seamless and immersive "phygital" experience. Marketers can leverage this approach to cater to the demands of the young generations of customers who are phygital natives.

Defining Spatial Marketing

Spatial marketing seeks to emulate the human ability of situational awareness, a crucial aspect of in-person experiences. In traditional brick-and-mortar settings, understanding customers, providing personalized offers, and creating interactive engagements require human intervention. As a result, frontline workers play a significant role in making informed decisions based on their understanding of the environment and the customers they serve.

To automate these processes, spatial marketing combines three emerging marketing concepts: proximity marketing, contextual marketing, and augmented marketing (refer to Figure 9.2). Proximity marketing enables marketers to identify the presence of customers in physical locations. By leveraging this spatial awareness, marketers can utilize contextual marketing to deliver relevant content at the right

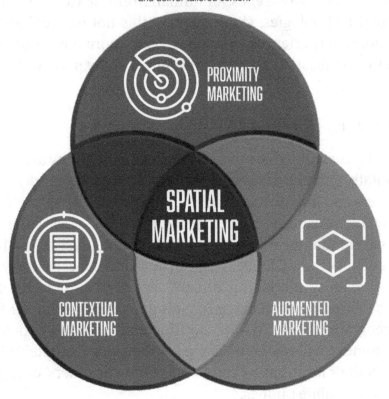

LEVERAGING SPATIAL COMPUTING FOR MARKETING

Identify customer location
and deliver tailored content

PROXIMITY
MARKETING

SPATIAL
MARKETING

CONTEXTUAL
MARKETING

AUGMENTED
MARKETING

Offering the right product at the
right moment in the right place

Delivering digital experiences
in physical environments

FIGURE 9.2   What Is Spatial Marketing?

moment and in the appropriate location. Additionally, augmented marketing enhances real-life experiences by integrating virtual elements, resulting in a more captivating and immersive overall customer experience.

By combining these approaches, marketers can replicate the situational awareness of human frontline workers using digital technologies. Consequently, this not only enhances customer experiences by making them more novel but also enables consistent and scalable delivery of experiences.

Proximity Marketing

The success of spatial marketing relies on the ability to enable digitally enhanced physical spaces to recognize nearby customers and initiate meaningful interactions with them. This is where proximity marketing comes into play, serving as a powerful tool for marketers to identify the precise location of customers and deliver customized content accordingly.

Proximity marketing utilizes location-based technologies, including geofencing (creating a virtual perimeter for a geographic area), Wi-Fi, and Bluetooth beacons, to detect customers' whereabouts. These technologies accurately pinpoint their locations by connecting with customers' devices, such as mobile phones.

In retail settings, companies can also determine customers' locations when they use their mobile phones to scan quick-response (QR) codes or interact with near-field communication (NFC) tags placed in specific sections to access product information. As a result, many retailers incorporate QR codes on product tags or equip them with NFC chips.

Another approach to determining a customer's presence in a particular location involves using AI-powered face recognition technology. For example, some retailers employ face detection cameras that can only identify demographic profiles of customers, such as the smart coolers at Walgreens, which deduce shoppers' age and gender to recommend specific cold drinks. On the other hand, Bestore, a snack food chain in China, utilizes Alibaba's facial recognition technology to identify particular individuals in its database and recommend products based on their historical purchases.

Using AI-powered cameras allows companies to detect customers' moods and emotions by analyzing their facial expressions and body language. This is useful for delivering targeted ads with the right tone for customers' states of mind. For example, many digital out-of-home (OOH) billboards are equipped with cameras to detect the audience's demographic and mood to personalize the displayed ads.

For instance, JCDecaux, an OOH advertising company, has created a digital billboard in Australia that can detect facial expressions and estimate the emotions of passersby. This innovative technology was utilized in the "Fix your Hanger" campaign for Yoplait Yoghurt Smoothie. The billboards determine the audience's moods and dispense suitable vouchers based on their emotions.

However, addressing the privacy concerns associated with proximity marketing is crucial. It should operate on a permission-based model, allowing customers to grant or deny companies the ability to track their locations or store their facial information. When implemented with these ethical considerations in mind, proximity marketing enables marketers to deliver more effective offers.

Many retailers, including Walmart, Target, Kroger, Macy's, and CVS, have embraced proximity marketing due to its wide range of uses, particularly in delivering location-specific advertising messages nearby and within their physical locations. One notable benefit is the ability to drive foot traffic to stores. Customers in close proximity to a store can receive notifications on their smartphone apps regarding promotional offers and directions to the store.

Furthermore, proximity marketing facilitates in-store advertisements. Retailers can track customers as they navigate different aisles and sections of the store. When retailers detect that customers spend more time in a particular location, indicating interest in a specific product, they can automatically deliver tailored promotions. These location-specific offers have proven to be more effective in driving purchase conversion.

Proximity marketing also plays a significant role in product discovery and assisting customers with in-store navigation. Retailers can integrate proximity marketing into their mobile apps, creating digital in-store maps that make it easier for customers to locate specific items on their shopping lists and see their real-time proximity to those products.

Moreover, proximity marketing enables retailers to gather valuable insights into customer behavior, such as the time spent in-store, the routes taken within the store, and the effectiveness of in-store promotions. This information proves useful for retailers in improving product assortments, enhancing store layouts and visual displays, and designing more effective product promotions.

Contextual Marketing

Another crucial aspect of spatial marketing is the implementation of personalized interactions, commonly referred to as contextual marketing. This strategy is widely utilized in online advertising, where advertisements are tailored to closely align with the content of the web page being viewed by the audience.

To achieve this, a contextual marketing system employs an algorithm that understands the online environment in which the audience is engaged. By analyzing the content they are consuming, the system identifies and presents ad inventories that match the themes of that content. For example, viewers of a car review video may see commercials for car accessories, while readers of a sports news site may encounter ads for a sporting goods store.

With the integration of digital technologies into physical spaces through spatial marketing, it is now possible to implement contextual marketing in real-world environments. Proximity marketing plays a crucial role in gathering extensive customer information, including their identities, demographics, current location, and shopping behaviors. To enrich this data, companies can integrate additional databases to enable the backend AI to understand the true context better.

Once the customer's identity is identified, AI can access the loyalty program database to retrieve their historical purchase data. By utilizing AI algorithms, companies can comprehend the customer's relationship with them and evaluate the potential for cross-selling and up-selling opportunities. Companies can suggest the most suitable products and relevant content based on this analysis.

For example, a grocery retailer can predict which regular groceries each shopper will likely run out of and when based on their previous purchases and suggest these items for restocking. Moreover, they can recommend products that complement each other. A sporting goods store, for example, can recommend a can of tennis balls to customers who have previously purchased rackets. Likewise, a department store can offer children's sunscreen products to customers who have bought swimming diapers.

Additionally, companies can incorporate external environmental information, such as current events, time of day, and weather conditions. For instance, select McDonald's stores and drive-throughs utilize digital menu boards that dynamically change based on traffic, time of day, and weather. The menu will display weather-appropriate items, such as McFlurries and shakes during hot weather, and cappuccino or hot chocolate during cold weather. When customers order something salty, the menu might recommend a soda to balance it out. During peak traffic times, the display could offer a quick menu to expedite service and minimize queue times at the drive-through.

In the past, delivering a contextual experience in physical spaces relied on frontline staff's ability to read their customers by paying attention to their needs and nonverbal cues. Some staff members might recognize customers and have prior interactions, which enables them to provide personalized service. Staff members also need to be knowledgeable about the products to recommend the best ones to customers. However, despite its effectiveness, this approach is not efficient. Nowadays, this practice can be automated, enabling mass customization.

Augmented Marketing

As businesses prioritize in-person experiences, they increasingly turn to spatial computing to elevate the customer journey within physical spaces. By leveraging spatial computing, companies can introduce an additional layer of digital engagement that complements the physical experience. This concept is called augmented marketing.

One practical approach to achieve this is utilizing technology to enrich the product experience, recognizing that customers now place greater value on experiential aspects than the products themselves. A notable example is the use of augmented reality (AR) by beauty and fashion retailers, enabling customers to try on makeup and apparel products virtually while shopping online. Through this technology, customers can visualize how different products appear on their bodies, aiding their decision-making process.

Retailers have extended this immersive experience to their physical stores as well. For instance, Sephora has implemented virtual try-on capabilities for lipsticks, eyeshadows, and eyeliners. This empowers customers to explore a broader range of products before selecting the ones they wish to test in person, simplifying the selection process. Additionally, this approach offers an educational and entertaining way for customers to discover products that best suit their preferences, ultimately increasing their willingness to pay.

Businesses can also enhance in-store customer engagement by encouraging interaction with the physical space. For example, retailers can introduce gamification experiences like scavenger hunts, where customers collect points by interacting with different store sections. Furthermore, interactive digital displays featuring touchscreen or gesture control technology enable customers to engage with digital content inside the store.

A prime example of this approach is Burberry's social retail store in China, which seamlessly integrates social media into the in-store experience. The luxury brand incentivizes customers to use WeChat, a popular social media platform, to explore the store's products, each equipped with scannable QR code tags. When customers scan these tags, they can access product storytelling content on the store's digital screens and their own mobile devices. Additionally, customers earn points with each interactive activity, which they can redeem for various benefits.

The store also features an interactive store window that not only showcases the brand's fashion collection but also adapts to the shopper's body shape and responds to their movements. This dynamic display creates a unique and personalized visual experience that shoppers can capture and share on their social media platforms, further amplifying the brand's reach and creating a sense of exclusivity.

Selfridges in London is another example of augmented marketing. They have transformed the traditional mannequin displays commonly seen in fashion stores. Instead, their store window uses digital technology. The digital windows showcase artistic 3D-animated representations of the products sold in the store. Moreover, the window is shoppable, allowing customers to purchase directly by scanning QR codes for the featured items.

Spatial marketing enables companies to deliver physical interactions that are augmented with digital experiences. It provides an entirely immersive customer experience, allowing interaction with products and elements in physical stores. By incorporating a virtual layer, companies enhance the customer journey, making it more convenient, entertaining, and interactive.

Implementing Spatial Marketing

To successfully integrate digital experiences into physical retail environments, businesses must follow a three-step process (see Figure 9.3). They must first understand customers' pain points. These pain points often include difficulties in product discovery and a tedious purchasing process. By observing these challenges, companies can identify opportunities to enhance the customer experience.

The next step is determining how spatial marketing can address these pain points. Marketers can draw inspiration from e-commerce and apply digital tools such as QR codes, augmented reality, and proximity sensors to improve product discovery and create engaging experiences. However, assessing the feasibility and desirability of these solutions is crucial before implementing them. Companies must evaluate their capabilities, resources, and return on investment while ensuring that these digital experiences provide value to customers.

DEVELOPING SPATIAL MARKETING CAPABILITIES

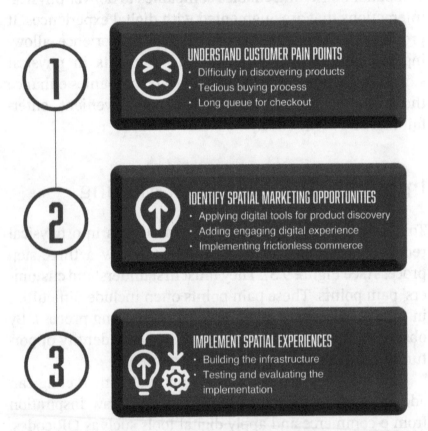

FIGURE 9.3 Three Steps of Spatial Marketing Design.

Once the feasibility and desirability are established, companies can implement spatial experiences, starting with pilot projects. This iterative approach allows marketers to find the best balance between delivering exceptional customer experiences and achieving great financial results.

Understand Customer Pain Points

Many businesses adopt technology merely to appear trendy and offer a unique experience. However, it is important to recognize that the primary purpose of adopting technology should always be to address customer problems. Similarly, when integrating digital experiences into physical interactions, it is crucial to start by identifying the challenges faced by customers and then strategizing how technology can effectively resolve those issues.

Companies must begin by observing the pain points of purely physical touchpoints. In brick-and-mortar settings, the most common pain point is the difficulty of discovering products. Most customers have issues finding specific items, especially in big-box retailers with broad product assortments.

E-commerce addresses this issue by implementing a search function and personalized recommendations. A robust search tool assists customers with specific items in mind, enabling them to locate and make purchases quickly. Conversely, personalized recommendations cater to customers who are browsing without particular needs, suggesting relevant products based on their interests.

Consequently, customers who shop online do not encounter the same difficulties in discovering products, even when faced with a vast assortment. Therefore, integrating digital experiences that replicate the product discovery process in e-commerce can benefit customers. Furthermore, implementing such digital features makes sense for companies as it improves the overall customer experience and satisfaction.

Another common pain point is the tedious purchasing process often associated with in-person shopping. In some categories, like regular groceries, customers demand convenience since it is typically considered a chore. Therefore, they aim to complete their shopping as quickly as possible with minimal hassle.

Conversely, customers seek something exciting and engaging in different categories, such as fashion, consumer electronics, and furniture. The concept of retail therapy, which can make people happier by providing a perception of control and stimulating their senses, comes into play. However, frequently, even in these categories, the buying process turns out to be boring and transactional. Moreover, despite being able to touch and feel the products, customers face difficulty accessing additional information and comparing products, as they would in online shopping.

Another significant friction point in the in-store customer journey is the time-consuming checkout, where queues and waiting times often frustrate customers. This is in contrast to e-commerce, where the checkout experience is hassle-free and instant. The pandemic, which familiarized customers with online shopping, has especially increased their expectations that any transaction should be processed quickly.

It is important to note that customer pain points may vary across different industries and companies. Understanding these pain points is crucial in determining key priorities for improvement. This understanding will guide marketers in designing the best customer experience that seamlessly blends physical and digital touchpoints.

Identify Spatial Marketing Opportunities

The next step involves determining how spatial marketing can address specific customer pain points. Since many of these pain points arise from rising customer expectations in online shopping experiences, marketers can draw inspiration from e-commerce and apply it to brick-and-mortar channels.

Marketers need to explore various solutions and evaluate their qualities. For instance, if the pain point relates to product discovery, digital tools can be employed to assist customers in finding products. Simple solutions may include incorporating QR codes on products or introducing augmented reality (AR) experiences to enhance the product discovery process. Another solution is using proximity sensors to guide customers in navigating the store, offering recommendations as they approach specific sections or helping them locate products accurately.

To ensure a seamless experience, a mobile app with all these features is essential. The app should have an in-store mode that enables customers to scan QR codes and access AR features. In addition, it should integrate with in-store sensors to facilitate proximity marketing and in-store navigation.

Alternatively, if customer frustration stems from a desire for engaging experiences, marketers should consider incorporating fun elements within the store. This can be achieved through in-store gamification or interactive displays. For instance, fashion retailers can utilize virtual fitting rooms to provide customers with more exciting and novel experiences while selecting the best-fitting clothes.

When the challenge lies in the checkout and payment process, potential solutions may include implementing self-service checkouts where customers can scan their shopping cart and automatically pay with pre-saved payment methods. A more advanced solution could involve adopting Amazon's "Just Walk Out" payment system, allowing customers to select items, leave the store, and have their payment method charged after exiting.

Marketers must assess the feasibility of the solutions. They need to determine whether their companies have the necessary capabilities and resources to develop these digital solutions that guide customers throughout their in-store journeys. Additionally, they must evaluate the return on investment of installing these technological infrastructures.

Furthermore, it is equally crucial to assess whether customers find using and engaging with these digital experiences desirable. Marketers must ensure that these solutions do not generate new pain points but provide value to the customers.

Implement Spatial Experiences

Assessing the desirability of spatial experiences is often challenging for companies, as it requires experimenting with digital solutions. To determine whether these new customer experiences will be successful and justify their investments, companies must take a leap and make initial investments to establish the necessary infrastructure.

The development of infrastructure for comprehensive spatial experiences can be a costly endeavor. For example, spatial marketing entails the implementation of a smart sensor infrastructure, which may involve installing various technologies such as beacons or facial recognition cameras throughout the store. These sensors play a crucial role in capturing data and providing personalized experiences to customers. However, installing and maintaining such infrastructure requires a significant financial commitment.

Similarly, incorporating interactive displays, such as digital store windows or virtual fitting rooms, also demands substantial financial resources. These immersive elements enhance the customer experience by offering innovative ways to engage with products. However, their installation involves hardware, software, and content creation expenses.

Considering the high costs involved, it is understandable that many companies approach implementing spatial marketing solutions cautiously. To mitigate risk and control expenses, companies often opt to pilot their answers on a smaller scale, typically starting with their flagship stores. These stores represent the brand's identity and serve as a showcase for new initiatives. By testing the spatial experiences in these stores, companies can evaluate the customer response and gather valuable insights before scaling up to a more significant number of locations.

The pilot phase allows companies to assess the effectiveness of the infrastructure and the impact of spatial experiences on customer behavior. It provides an opportunity to fine-tune the technology, address any challenges that arise, and make data-driven decisions based on the feedback received. This iterative approach helps companies optimize their investments and align their strategies with the preferences and expectations of their target audience.

Ultimately, the goal is to strike a balance between innovation and financial feasibility. By piloting spatial experiences in select locations, companies can gather evidence of their desirability and assess whether the potential benefits outweigh the costs. This prudent approach enables companies to make informed decisions and confidently expand spatial marketing initiatives across their retail footprint.

Summary: Delivering Natural Human-Machine Interactions

In recent decades, the way humans interact with machines has transitioned to touchscreens, and with advancing technology, machines are increasingly emulating human capabilities. Spatial marketing takes advantage of this trend by integrating physical interactions with intuitive digital experiences.

Spatial computing enhances proximity marketing, enabling marketers to detect customers' presence and deliver tailored messages. It also leverages contextual marketing, which allows marketers to provide personalized value propositions to customers powered by AI. Ultimately, spatial marketing is about blending physical and digital experiences by augmenting the real world with digital content and interactions.

REFLECTION QUESTIONS

- How can your company leverage spatial marketing to enhance customer experiences within physical locations? For example, how do you establish the necessary infrastructure to identify customers and provide personalized offers? Furthermore, what digital experiences can you integrate into the physical space?

- How do you ensure that privacy concerns are effectively addressed during collecting and analyzing customer data for spatial marketing? What are some of the other challenges that may arise during the implementation of spatial marketing?

CHAPTER 10

Metaverse Marketing

Experimenting with the Next-Generation Engagement

Numerous brands have embraced marketing within the metaverse, capitalizing on the unique opportunities it offers to engage customers in a three-dimensional, virtual space. This form of marketing is seen as a fresh approach, expanding beyond traditional two-dimensional marketing in social media and other content platforms. Within virtual worlds, brands can explore remarkably creative endeavors that would be otherwise impossible in physical spaces, such as hosting a 10-minute-only concert or offering instantly customizable sneakers.

Moreover, the metaverse is a powerful platform for captivating an emerging audience, specifically younger demographics who are highly accustomed to virtual exploration. For metaverse natives—Generation Z and Generation Alpha—spending extended periods in virtual worlds is a familiar and natural experience. To them, the metaverse represents an immersive fusion of video games and social media.

To stay relevant in the next decade, brands entering the metaverse must either have a significant portion of their existing customer base composed of Generation Z and Generation Alpha or actively engage with these demographics to secure them as future customers. Therefore, these brands must identify the intersections between the metaverse natives and their desired target audience. They should only establish a presence in the metaverse if this overlap is sizeable enough to justify the necessary investments.

Certain brands appear to be jumping on the metaverse bandwagon solely due to the fear of missing out. As the initial excitement surrounding the metaverse subsides, these brands look lost and uncertain. In the face of challenging economic conditions, they opt to reduce their investments in metaverse marketing. Without clear objectives and a well-defined roadmap, these brands risk wasting resources in pursuit of short-term gains.

In previous chapters, we have established that the metaverse is indeed a long-term investment for brands and may not yield immediate results. Nevertheless, there is overwhelming evidence suggesting that the metaverse holds immense potential. The movement is aligned with demographic shifts toward the younger generations. Furthermore, digital trends and enabling technologies converge toward immersive marketing, making it an inevitable path for businesses to embrace.

Some brands remain committed to the metaverse, striving to become pioneers in this emerging realm. They have a good understanding of the key success factors (see Figure 10.1). They know that metaverse marketing is not meant to replace traditional marketing in physical spaces but rather to complement it. As a result, they seamlessly integrate their metaverse initiatives into their existing marketing strategies, ensuring the sustainability of their metaverse marketing efforts.

Successful brands in the metaverse focus on engaging the existing metaverse communities, such as those found in Roblox and Fortnite. These communities of young gamers and creators have already established a thriving ecosystem within the metaverse. As a result, marketing efforts targeted toward these communities have proven effective, gaining traction and generating significant interest. However, attracting new adopters poses more challenges.

KEYS TO SUCCESSFUL METAVERSE MARKETING

FIGURE 10.1   Key Success Factors of Metaverse Marketing.

Successful brand campaigns in the metaverse place a strong emphasis on simplicity to attract new customers. They eliminate the need for costly devices such as virtual reality headsets and controllers, making participation accessible through any computer or Internet-connected device.

In addition, brands cater to new users who may not be avid gamers by providing experiences that prioritize social connections, enabling users to interact and connect with others in virtual environments similar to social media platforms. Moreover, the popularity of virtual clothing for avatars has soared due to its simplicity.

These successful brands also recognize that the metaverse, especially the decentralized version, may suffer from an image issue associated with non-fungible tokens (NFTs) and cryptocurrencies—as elaborated in Chapter 5—which currently have unfavorable perceptions. While they leverage blockchain technology in their metaverse ventures, most brands that successfully release virtual products refrain from explicitly labeling their collections as NFTs, primarily due to the negative perception surrounding them. Some of these brands even choose to steer clear of decentralized metaverses entirely and instead opt for the more widely accepted centralized versions.

Above all, companies that have successfully experimented in the metaverse adhere to a well-defined road map. It begins with understanding the target audiences—their motivations and objectives—within this virtual realm. By understanding these factors, brands can tailor their offerings to meet the specific needs of these customers, creating real value rather than merely following trends. Brands must also carefully select the most suitable implementation avenue, considering the diverse metaverse options available, each with its characteristics and governance structures (see Figure 10.2).

PLANNING FOR METAVERSE MARKETING

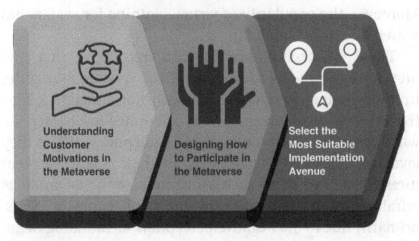

Understanding Customer Motivations in the Metaverse

Designing How to Participate in the Metaverse

Select the Most Suitable Implementation Avenue

FIGURE 10.2 Three Steps of Metaverse Marketing.

Understanding Customer Motivations in the Metaverse

For most young generations, the metaverse serves as a virtual refuge from the challenges of the real world. Many also view the metaverse as an opportunity to connect with others and engage in social interactions with a sense of freedom. Moreover, a growing number of users consider the metaverse a viable alternative to conventional e-commerce platforms. Finally, a group of creators perceives the metaverse as a platform for financial gain, utilizing play-to-earn mechanisms, creating virtual products, and participating in the metaverse's creator economy (see Figure 10.3).

FIGURE 10.3 Customer Motivations to Participate in the Metaverse.

Metaverse as a Fun Escape

Sometimes, everyday life can be a bit overwhelming. That is when people seek a brief escape from their routines and engage in activities such as playing video games, scrolling through social media, or going on trips.

The metaverse combines all these enjoyable aspects: users can play games, explore content, and even travel within it. It serves as a perfect way to take a break and offers a welcome distraction from the stresses of everyday life. A global survey by Oliver Wyman confirmed that 41 percent of users cited a fun experience as the key reason they participate in the metaverse.

The metaverse is indeed a fun and relaxing space where individuals can freely express themselves using avatars. They have the power to choose their appearance and decide how to spend their time without worrying about what others think. It is like being able to embody better versions of themselves.

The metaverse is an immersive experience where players feel genuinely part of a virtual world. It gives them a sense of purpose and meaning as they navigate through it. Thus, people can get lost in the metaverse for hours, only to return the next day and continue where they left off.

Moreover, the metaverse adds excitement by incorporating elements of role-playing games, including missions and competitions. Unlike complex video games, metaverse gaming often follows a more straightforward gameplay. This simplicity is essential as it provides a sense of achievement and challenge that keeps players engaged.

One of the remarkable aspects of the metaverse is that it allows limitless imagination. It opens up endless possibilities and takes users to new and exciting places. It is designed to reflect the physical world, yet it also grants people the freedom to invent and dream big. Moreover, the metaverse enables individuals to develop skills and pursue creative interests that they may not have the opportunity to explore in real life. So whether it is becoming a successful entrepreneur, an imaginative architect, a skilled coder, or an adventurous hunter, the metaverse offers avenues for these pursuits.

Metaverse as a Space to Connect

Another reason people are motivated to use the metaverse is to establish relationships with others. Approximately 26 percent of metaverse natives look for connection when participating in the metaverse (Oliver Wyman). However, it is important to emphasize that the metaverse is not meant to replace in-person interactions when building relationships. Instead, it represents the next phase of digital communication.

Undoubtedly, the metaverse offers the closest approximation to real-life interactions within the digital realm. While social media enables asynchronous communication, allowing for conversations to be paused and resumed at will, the metaverse operates on a synchronous interaction model, facilitating real-time exchanges between individuals. Within the metaverse, people can share experiences simultaneously.

Although instant messaging also allows for synchronous communication, the metaverse distinguishes itself by providing a three-dimensional environment where individuals can socialize in virtual settings. These immersive environments offer a genuine sense of social presence, incorporating appearances, body language, and spatial awareness, resulting in a higher level of immersion. In essence, the metaverse can be seen as an inhabitable Internet where encounters with others constantly occur due to user proximity within the virtual space.

Communities thrive in the metaverse due to a phenomenon known as media multiplexity. This concept states that individuals with strong bonds tend to connect through various communication methods, particularly digital channels. As a result, communities that already share close relationships through other media naturally gravitate toward the metaverse.

Additionally, the metaverse contributes to developing stronger bonds among community members. Since the metaverse involves interacting in different spaces with specific storylines or gameplays, users often collaborate in navigating these environments. Each individual assumes a unique role in pursuing common goals, fostering a more profound sense of connection and collaboration.

Metaverse for Convenient Shopping

Just as social media transformed into a platform for social commerce, allowing people to shop directly on social media storefronts, the metaverse is poised to become the next stage in the evolution of e-commerce. Present-day meta-verses already possess their own economies and can facil-itate transactions, thus enabling digital commerce within their virtual realms.

Within the metaverse, everyone can construct their own digital spaces. Therefore, companies are developing digital replicas of their physical stores, effectively transforming the metaverse into a more immersive variation of an e-commerce platform. The shopping experience in this virtual realm depends on the product categories, but it can offer highly imaginative elements that exceed the limitations of physical locations.

Metaverse inhabitants have already embraced the con-cept of shopping within the virtual realm. According to a study by Obsess, one-third of customers have expressed interest in engaging in metaverse commerce. Nevertheless, since not all product categories, such as food and beverages, can be virtually consumed, metaverse commerce will need to pair the metaverse experience with real-world touchpoints.

Metaverse enables users to engage in virtual shopping within digital stores and seamlessly continue their experi-ence in physical locations. For instance, customers can earn points by participating in gameplay within virtual restaurants and later redeem those points for actual food and beverages at brick-and-mortar establishments.

Moreover, customers can immerse themselves in immersive product try-on and customization experiences, particularly in virtual apparel stores. Avatar salespeople are available to assist shoppers in finding items and offer-ing product recommendations based on their preferences.

Once customers discover the products they desire, they can place orders directly within the virtual stores and have the products delivered to their home addresses. Integrating metaverse experiences with in-person experiences is the ideal model for metaverse natives.

Metaverse for Financial Gain

Early adopters of the metaverse are far from passive partici-pants, as many embrace the mission of customer empower-ment in Web3. Instead, they build communities of metaverse natives, actively collaborating to construct a thriving busi-ness ecosystem within virtual worlds. These early adopters, such as gamers, investors, creators, and service providers, assume specific roles within the ecosystem.

The metaverse presents numerous opportunities for them to earn income. For instance, some metaverses offer a play-to-earn model. In this model, gamers can engage in spe-cific activities aligned with the game mechanics, complete quests, and get various forms of digital currency, which can later be converted into real money.

Investing in and trading digital assets is another ave-nue for earning money within the metaverse. For example, some investors purchase and sell virtual lands at higher prices. They can also develop them into rentable spaces. This process is akin to real estate development but within virtual realms.

The metaverse is also a haven for user-generated con-tent. Creators focus on crafting virtual products, such as avatar accessories, that can be sold on metaverse marketplaces.

Furthermore, creators can develop games within established metaverses and monetize them by charging for game access and offering in-game accessories. Additionally, creators can build their businesses by designing spaces and selling products.

The services industry is also flourishing within the metaverse. Users can host events such as concerts and seminars, selling tickets to participants. They can also offer virtual tours and sell experiences. Furthermore, some users become virtual influencers, recommending products and services to their loyal followers in the metaverse and earning commissions, similar to affiliate marketing. These commercial endeavors within the metaverse provide additional avenues for financial gain.

Designing How to Participate in the Metaverse

By understanding the primary drivers behind their target audience's participation in the metaverse, businesses can determine the most effective approach for entering this virtual realm and offering unique value propositions. It may include introducing branded collectibles, crafting immersive advertising experiences, establishing online-to-offline commerce channels, and implementing gamified loyalty programs. Brands can undertake multiple metaverse initiatives, depending on their available resources and overarching objectives (see Figure 10.4).

FIGURE 10.4 How Brands Participate in the Metaverse.

Launch Branded Collectibles

To effectively connect with metaverse natives seeking fun escapes, brands can begin by introducing their branded collectibles. This approach effectively communicates the brand's understanding and appeal to younger audiences. Moreover, it allows brands to exhibit their playful and trendy nature since the metaverse provides a unique opportunity for marketers to create digital replicas of products that would otherwise be impossible to develop in the physical realm.

The younger generations like collecting, but their preferences differ. Generation Y enjoys amassing collections that build their social status and evoke nostalgia from their childhood, such as retro sneakers, sports cards, and McDonald's Happy Meal toys. On the other hand, Generation Z and Generation Alpha are more inclined to collect items centered around experiences. Therefore, when it comes to virtual collectibles, the emphasis should not be on ownership but rather on the experiential attribute.

Let us consider an analogy to illustrate this distinction. Generation Y may have found joy in collecting physical Pokémon cards as they grew up. In contrast, Generation Z and Generation Alpha derive satisfaction from the thrill of traveling to different locations to pursue collectible monsters in the Pokémon Go game. Similarly, virtual avatar accessories are not merely about possessing virtual sneakers and jackets but rather about the experience of customizing avatars to reflect their identity.

Generation Y has a penchant for exclusivity when it comes to collectibles, as they are highly motivated by the scarcity of items. On the contrary, for Generation Z and

Generation Alpha, collecting is like an entry ticket to be part of communities and tribes with the same passions and interests. Therefore, they prefer collectibles that are more inclusive.

An example of a brand that has ventured into virtual collectibles is Nike's Jordan brand, which has released various virtual sneakers such as Air Jordan 1 and Air Jordan XI in Fortnite. These virtual items are accompanied by in-game interactive challenges where players can perform some activities to win Jordan-branded skins.

In a decentralized metaverse, collectibles are powered by NFTs. These NFTs enable collectibles to include rights to various experiences and memberships within specific communities. Think of these collectibles as virtual membership cards. Consequently, virtual collectibles go beyond mere face value and have the potential to possess real-world value, especially when linked to physical experiences and community engagements.

One example is Nike's virtual community for sports enthusiasts, called .SWOOSH, which requires users to collaboratively create virtual creations to become members and gain access to local community events and experiences. These collectibles act as portals to a fun escape, fulfilling the desires of metaverse inhabitants in both the digital and physical realms.

Develop Experiential Advertising

Since the virtual world mirrors the real world, it is easy to envision that advertising opportunities in the metaverse are

Designing How to Participate in the Metaverse   **225**

akin to those in reality. Imagine, for instance, out-of-home (OOH) ads on billboards and bus exteriors, but within virtual worlds. This type of in-game advertising is prevalent in video games, such as the presence of Nissin Cup Noodles ads on a truck in *Final Fantasy 15*, Mercedes-Benz cars as options to drive in *Mario Kart 8*, or a Verizon billboard in the *Alan Wake* game.

However, advertising in the metaverse exhibits some differences. Metaverse natives—Generation Y and Generation Alpha—are less receptive to traditional advertising, where brands simply place their logos and product advertisements within virtual worlds. Brands must adapt their advertising approach by integrating branded touchpoints into the immersive metaverse experience.

In contrast to conventional video games, the metaverse offers a unique opportunity for brands to construct dedicated spaces showcasing their products or services, enabling customers to engage and interact with the brands in immersive ways. Roblox, a metaverse highly favored by younger generations, refers to this as "immersive ads," which enable brands to transport players to branded virtual realms through 3D portals. A notable example is Van's branded virtual skatepark on Roblox, where players can personalize their virtual skates and dress their avatars in customized apparel while enjoying a skateboarding experience within the park.

Similarly, Samsung develops a metaverse experience to advertise their products to Generation Z by bringing *The Tonight Show starring Jimmy Fallon* to Fortnite. The setting features a digital twin of NBC Studio 6B at Rockefeller

Plaza, the actual filming location of the show. Fortnite gamers can play minigames inspired by the show as they discover the virtual space. Notably, Samsung's best-selling mobile products are prominently featured as power-ups, enabling gamers to level up their gameplay.

Branded spaces also serve as a means for brands to provide venues for communities to gather and build connections. By facilitating social connections, brands can effectively promote their advertising campaigns and establish trust. An example of this can be seen with The Home Depot, which offers a "Virtual Kids Workshop" on the popular platform Roblox, widely embraced by Generation Alpha.

Interested participants can explore The Home Depot's virtual store, where the kids can embark on an exciting scavenger hunt through the store aisles to find the necessary materials. Once collected, they can assemble virtual items, such as a birdhouse, a flower garden, or a car, and utilize these creations within the Roblox environment. This kind of experience fosters connections between customers and brands and strengthens the bonds among metaverse communities, which proves highly beneficial for brands.

Build Online-to-Offline (O2O) Commerce

The most significant limitation of the metaverse is that many product categories lack virtual experiences that can match the satisfaction of their real-world counterparts. For example, food and beverage companies cannot replicate the consumption experience in the metaverse. Similarly, while virtual clothing exists, it does not provide the same sensation as wearing real clothes.

This is not a novel challenge in the realm of e-commerce. Many omnichannel retailers employ the O2O model as a solution to integrate their digital and physical experiences seamlessly. For instance, these retailers attract prospective customers from online channels to visit their brick-and-mortar stores to complete their customer journey. A prevalent O2O strategy grocery and fashion retailers utilize is the "buy online, pick up in store" (BOPIS) service.

Brands can also adopt a similar O2O approach by linking and extending customers' immersive experiences within the metaverse to the real world. This strategy proves particularly effective in attracting younger generations who spend considerable time in the metaverse and offering them opportunities to extend their journey into the physical realm.

A noteworthy example is the virtual store of American Girl, which offers two distinct experiences. Kids can browse through virtual displays of the products, while adults can directly shop from the virtual store. Additionally, the brand has developed a virtual museum highlighting its rich heritage. The virtual store's resemblance to American Girl's Rockefeller Center store generates interest and lures customers to visit the flagship store. Furthermore, visitors to the virtual store can also make reservations for tables and parties at the American Girl Café through an integration with the store's reservation system, allowing them to extend their journey from the virtual realm to the physical location.

Drest, a metaverse focused on fashion styling, offers another compelling example. Users are presented with styling challenges involving celebrities and various events. By completing these tasks, they earn points and virtual currency that can be used to purchase new clothes within the metaverse. What makes Drest even more realistic is its collaboration with over 250 brands, including renowned names such as Gucci and Prada. Most importantly, users can order and purchase actual products featured in their virtual stylings directly from within the game, seamlessly integrating virtual and real-world fashion experiences.

Implement a Gamified Loyalty Program

The play-to-earn model within the metaverse serves as an inspiration for brands to engage customers who seek tangible incentives for their interactions. Brands can adopt a loyalty program that integrates elements of gamification and rewards. Customers are motivated to interact with these brands through immersive gameplay experiences, earning gifts that can be redeemed in the real world.

Chipotle has embraced this concept by venturing into the metaverse by introducing "Burrito Builder" on Roblox. Players are challenged with rolling virtual burritos in this virtual store reminiscent of Chipotle's original Denver location, capturing the nostalgic 1990s theme. As an exciting incentive, the first 100,000 players who complete this task will receive a virtual currency exchangeable for real-world food at Chipotle's physical restaurants. Through this campaign, Chipotle effectively merges the play-to-earn model of the metaverse with real-world activations in its physical establishments.

Another compelling example is Starbucks Odyssey, which has launched NFT-powered collectible stamps for customers to acquire and redeem for various digital and physical experiences. This innovative concept shares similarities with Starbucks' renowned loyalty program, Starbucks Rewards, but incorporates NFT technology and immersive experiences to provide a unique twist.

Furthermore, using NFT technology enables companies and customer communities to co-create digital products and sell them in marketplaces. This value proposition resonates with a subset of metaverse natives motivated by the creator economy inherent in the metaverse. Brands that facilitate this co-creation process with creators have the opportunity to forge strong bonds with these active customers.

Nike's .SWOOSH platform exemplifies this concept by encouraging members to engage in community challenges and jointly develop NFT-linked virtual products in partnership with Nike. This unique opportunity allows creators to earn royalties from the sales of the digital products they help create. By embracing this platform, Nike revolutionizes its design process while also strengthening its relationship with customers who are independent creators. The platform serves as a means to facilitate creators in earning income, fulfilling their motivation to engage in the metaverse.

Select the Most Suitable Implementation Avenue

When brands consider their participation in the metaverse, they carefully plan the best way to enter this virtual realm (see Figure 10.5). Customers who encounter familiar brands within the metaverse perceive them as pioneers and

IMPLEMENTING METAVERSE CAMPAIGN THE RIGHT WAY

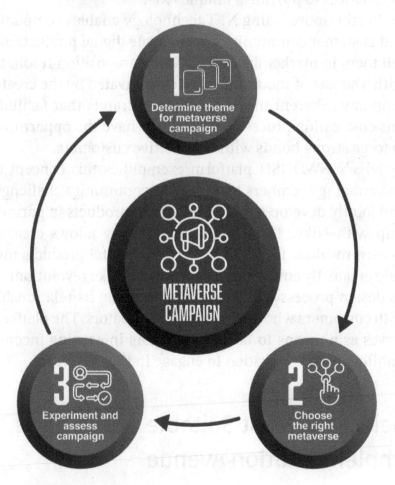

FIGURE 10.5 Implementing Metaverse Marketing.

innovators, raising their expectations significantly. However, bigger does not always mean better in the metaverse. Instead, brands must adopt a unique and differentiated theme that sets them apart from the existing metaverse experiences.

The best way for brands to achieve this is by maintaining their brand positioning and overall narrative from the real world when expanding their presence into the metaverse. For instance, Starbucks, known for providing a third-place experience and rewarding loyal customers, extends the same concept to its presence in the metaverse. Similarly, The Home Depot, focusing on do-it-yourself (DIY) projects, designs metaverse activations that revolve around this core theme.

It is also crucial to consider the choice of the metaverse. Numerous metaverses are currently available, and new ones will continue to emerge. Some brands even create their own metaverses on a smaller scale. The two existing types of metaverses—centralized and decentralized—offer distinct features for brands to leverage. As previously explained, currently, centralized metaverses are the most popular choice, primarily because they are not affected by the image problems associated with NFTs and cryptocurrencies.

However, centralized metaverses are predominantly oriented toward gaming communities, as they are often built on world-building game platforms like Roblox, Fortnite, and Minecraft. Even among these options, there are differences in user profiles. For instance, Roblox has a predominantly young user base, with a majority of its users being under 16 years old, while Fortnite attracts a slightly older demographic, with most users falling between the ages of 18 and 24.

On the other hand, decentralized metaverses, such as The Sandbox and Decentraland, offer enhanced functionality due to the implementation of blockchain technology. However, utilizing blockchain technology also carries certain risks, as it may be less familiar to average customers. Therefore, brands must select the right metaverse that aligns with the desired user profile.

Brands can experiment with various themes and metaverses by creating limited-time campaigns to gauge audience interest and reception. Gucci serves as an example of a brand exploring multiple metaverse campaigns. First, the luxury fashion brand introduced the Gucci Garden, a temporary virtual space available for two weeks in Roblox. It also organized a two-week activation event called the Gucci Vault Land in The Sandbox. Eventually, Gucci established a permanent presence in Roblox with a dedicated space called Gucci Town.

To measure the success of metaverse entry, brands can consider metrics such as the number of users participating in the campaign, brand lift in terms of improved awareness and perception, and even incremental revenue generated. After evaluating these metrics and determining the ideal model for metaverse activations, brands can establish a more permanent presence in the metaverse.

Summary: Experimenting with the Next-Generation Engagement

The metaverse presents a potential platform for captivating an emerging audience, specifically Generation Z and

Generation Alpha. To these generations, the metaverse holds various meanings. It can be perceived as a fun escape, a space for fostering connections with others, an immersive form of e-commerce, or a platform for content creators to monetize their digital creations.

By comprehending the needs of this audience, brands can determine the optimal experience to offer within the metaverse. This may encompass branded collectibles, experiential advertising, seamless integration of online-to-offline commerce, and loyalty programs with gamified elements. Brands must engage in experimentation and exploration to uncover the most effective implementation model before committing more extensive resources to metaverse marketing.

REFLECTION QUESTIONS

- What are some potential benefits and drawbacks of the metaverse as a platform for engaging Generation Z and Generation Alpha? How do you think brands can navigate these considerations to create meaningful experiences?
- Is your company inclined to embrace the metaverse at an early stage of its development, or does it prefer to wait for the platforms to mature before establishing a presence in the metaverse?

Acknowledgments

The authors express their sincere gratitude to the leadership team at M Corp for their valuable support throughout the process of writing the book: Michael Hermawan, Jacky Mussry, Taufik, Vivie Jericho, Ence, Estania Rimadini, and Yosanova Savitry.

A special thanks goes to the Marketeers team: Marthani, Sigit, Hafiz, Aji, and Sanny, who have supplied the authors with great marketing knowledge and beautiful illustrating skills for the book's content.

We would also like to thank the editorial team at Wiley—Deborah Schindlar, Victoria Savanh, and Kelly Talbot—for the great collaboration during the development of Marketing 6.0.

About the Authors

Philip Kotler is professor emeritus of marketing at the Kellogg School of Management, where he held the S.C. Johnson & Son Professorship of International Marketing. *The Wall Street Journal* ranks him among the top six most influential business thinkers. The recipient of numerous awards and honorary degrees from schools worldwide, he holds an MA from the University of Chicago and a PhD from the Massachusetts Institute of Technology, both in economics. Philip has an incredible international presence—his books have been translated into more than 25 languages, and he regularly speaks on the international circuit.

Hermawan Kartajaya is the founder and chairman of M Corp. He has collaborated with Philip Kotler since 1998, coauthoring a remarkable collection of 12 books. He was named one of the "50 Gurus Who Have Shaped the Future of Marketing" by the Chartered Institute of Marketing, United Kingdom. Hermawan also received the Distinguished Global Leadership Award from the Pan-Pacific Business Association at the University of Nebraska–Lincoln. He is also the founder of the Asia Marketing Federation, the Asia Committee for Small Business, and the World Marketing Forum.

Iwan Setiawan is the chief executive officer of Marketeers, Indonesia's leading marketing media. He is also a marketing consultant with 20 years of experience, having helped over 100 clients across different industries. He teaches marketing for the Executive MBA program at the School of Business and Management, Bandung Institute of Technology (Jakarta, Indonesia). Iwan holds an MBA from the Kellogg School of Management at Northwestern University and a BEng from the University of Indonesia.

Index